THE STORY OF
WILLIAM & CATHERINE

THE PRINCE & PRINCESS OF WALES

Since his birth in 1982, Prince William's entire life has been mapped out – his education, his future role as king, his own line of succession. However, one thing nobody could have predicted was the future monarch falling head over heels in love with a beautiful – but profoundly un-royal – young woman named Catherine Middleton.

Despite growing up with drastically different childhoods, true love blossomed. *The Story of William & Catherine* reveals the highs and lows of a relationship that has survived over 20 years in the spotlight – from their low-key university romance and their bitter, high-profile break-up just years after their graduation, to how they rekindled their relationship and married in the ultimate fairytale wedding. Find out how Catherine has risen to the challenge of becoming a royal, and how the couple has used their global platform to raise awareness and champion causes close to their hearts.

CONTENTS

WILLIAM
Prince of Wales

008 .... A Prince is Born
012 .... The Heir and the Spare
018 .... An Education Fit for a King
022 .... Past-Times of a Young Prince
028 .... Royal Trips and Holidays
032 .... The Death of Diana
038 .... Raised in the Spotlight
042 .... Prince William at University
046 .... An Officer and a Gentleman
050 .... William's Charitable Contributions

CATHERINE
Princess of Wales

056 .... The Making of a Duchess
062 .... Student Days
070 .... Kate Goes to Work
074 .... Caring Kate's Causes and Charities

WILL & KATE
The Royal Couple

082 .... The Prince and the Commoner
094 .... William and Kate's Royal Wedding
104 .... The In-Laws
110 .... Keeping Up with the Cambridges
122 .... Modernising the Monarchy

WC

008	A Prince is Born
012	The Heir and the Spare
018	An Education Fit for a King
022	Past-Times of a Young Prince
028	Royal Trips and Holidays
032	The Death of Diana
038	Raised in the Spotlight
042	Prince William at University
046	An Officer and a Gentleman
050	William's Charitable Contributions

WILLIAM
Prince of Wales

A PRINCE is BORN

When Lady Diana Spencer gave birth to her eldest son, William, less than a year after marrying the Prince of Wales in July 1981, interest in the new members of the royal family reached fever pitch

It was a few days before her due date when Princess Diana went into labour with her first child and was whisked off to a private room in the Lindo Wing of St Mary's Hospital in Paddington at 5am, with Prince Charles at her side. As many first babies tend to arrive late, Diana had hoped that her child might be born on her own birthday, 1 July, but her son clearly had other ideas and made his appearance to the world at 9.03pm on 21 June, weighing a healthy 7lbs ½oz. The princess was in labour for 16 gruelling hours, supported by her husband, the first royal father to be present at the birth of his child, while Queen Elizabeth's own gynaecologist, George Pinker, who had looked after Diana during her pregnancy, presided over her labour.

The crowds were immense when the new baby prince, safely cradled in his mother's arms, made his public debut the following day before heading home to the couple's apartment in Kensington Palace, where Princess Margaret had organised a welcome reception for them. The news of his birth had been announced to an overjoyed nation the previous evening, by means of the traditional handwritten notice placed on an easel outside Buckingham Palace and, less formally, a banner across the bottom of television screens all across the country, interrupting a World Cup match. There was immediate speculation about what name would be chosen for the new prince, who had been referred to simply as 'Baby Wales' in hospital, with George being the even money favourite at bookmakers William Hill. Prince Charles teasingly informed the press that there were two main contenders for the new prince's name, but it would be exactly a week before Buckingham Palace announced that he

RIGHT Prince William was adored by both of his parents, who saw his birth as a chance to lay to rest the ghosts of their own unhappy childhoods and create the perfect, happy family life that they had both desperately longed for

was to be called William Arthur Philip Louis of Wales. The name William was enjoying something of a resurgence in popularity at the time, but also had the additional bonus of having a royal provenance as it was the name of four English kings. Arthur had a similarly medieval resonance and regal providence, while his other names were tributes to his grandfather, Philip, and his father's beloved late great-uncle Louis, Earl Mountbatten of Burma.

Prince William was baptised on 4 August 1982, the 82nd birthday of his great-grandmother, the Queen Mother, in the music room of Buckingham Palace by Robert Runcie, Archbishop of Canterbury. His godparents were King Constantine II of the Hellenes, Lord Romsey, Sir Laurens van der Post, Princess Alexandra, the Duchess of Westminster and Lady Susan Hussey. He wore the beautiful Spitalfields silk and Honiton lace christening robe that had been commissioned by Queen Victoria for her eldest daughter in 1841, and then worn by every royal baby until Queen Elizabeth commissioned a replica in 2008. The Princess of Wales was smiling and radiant in bright pink, which she wore

with the diamond and pearl necklace that her husband had given her after William's birth, but told friends later that she had felt overwhelmed and was in tears for most of the day.

Although delighted to be a mother, she was suffering from postnatal depression and anxious about her marriage, which was not the great romance that she had anticipated. Life with her baby was certainly not a disappointment, though, and she thoroughly enjoyed the time that she spent in the nursery, either at Kensington Palace or their country residence, Highgrove, in Wiltshire. The baby prince had a full-time nanny, Barbara 'Baba' Barnes, but like most royal mothers, Diana insisted upon breastfeeding her baby herself for several months and, along with Prince Charles, took great pride in doing as much as possible for him, although she had to grudgingly accept that her royal duties meant she was unable to spend as much time as she would have liked with her baby.

Diana had barely known Charles before their marriage, and although

> "*The princess is well and the baby's looking lovely. It's marvellous, he's not bad*"

FAR LEFT Diana insisted that William should accompany them on their tour of New Zealand and Australia, making him the first royal baby to do so. Except for this photo call in New Zealand, the little prince remained out of sight for most of the tour.

she was still desperate for his approval, she was also becoming increasingly disenchanted as it became more obvious that they had very little in common. He was nearly 13 years older, set in his ways, and could be extremely dull company. Much of this was down to personality, but Diana laid the blame squarely at the feet of his parents and was determined that she would not make the same mistakes with her own children. She saw herself as a royal rebel, forcing the stuffy establishment to become more modern and accessible, especially when it came to the upbringing of her children, whom she wanted to raise as normally as possible without any repressive stuffiness. Diana refurbished both of their homes to make them more comfortable, informal and modern, with particular attention paid to the rooms inhabited by the baby prince, which were filled with colour and stimulating toys and books. Before she married, Diana had loved working as a nanny and kindergarten teacher, and had very definite ideas about how she wanted her son to be raised. It seemed to her that her husband's upbringing had been rather sad and lonely, as his rank had precluded him from making many friends, and he had certainly never been allowed to befriend anyone outside a small, very tight-knit royal circle or have much contact with people from different backgrounds. Diana was determined that William would be raised very differently.

Even the occasional photo calls granted to the press were of a markedly less formal flavour than those of bygone days, when royal children would pose stiffly before the cameras,

barely bothering to conceal their discomfort and boredom. Instead, Diana would invite her favourite photographers to take photos of the family playing together. The results were warm, informal and affectionate, and made the Wales family appear approachable and just like any other couple with a lively baby. One of the most important photo shoots took place during the family's tour of Australia and New Zealand in spring 1983, when William was nine months old. It was the first time that a royal baby had accompanied their parents on tour – the presence of small children having previously been considered too distracting and inconvenient. The Queen and Prince Philip had always left their children behind when embarking on state visits but Diana, as always, was determined to do things her own way and insisted that William was too young to be left behind for six weeks. Although there were scheduled opportunities for the press and public to catch a glimpse of the little prince, he spent the majority of his time staying on a sheep station in Woomargama in New South Wales, with his devoted nanny Baba Barnes in attendance and frequent visits from his parents in between their numerous official engagements.

This trip to Australia underlined the fact that from now on Charles, Diana and their son were to be regarded as a team, a solid family unit, and that unlike the royal children of the past, who had been cared for solely by nannies and saw their parents for only a few minutes every day at teatime, William was being raised as a modern prince and was part of a normal, happy family. However, behind the perfect facade, all was not well in the Wales household, and despite the fact that the couple had expressed a wish to add to their family as quickly as possible, it was to be 18 months before they announced that another royal baby was on its way, and that Prince William would no longer be the sole resident of the royal nursery.

RIGHT As one of the most famous children in the world, William quickly developed a complicated and not altogether happy relationship with the press – as this photograph shows.

LEFT Another candid photo, taken just a couple of weeks before Christmas, where the family of three sit on a bench in their garden at Kensington Palace

Images: Getty

"The news of this particular royal baby was greeted with almost universal delight"

The HEIR and the SPARE

The arrival of Prince Harry in September 1984 completed the Wales family. Although their children had been born into a life of unimaginable privilege, Charles and Diana were keen for them to enjoy as normal an upbringing as possible

When the one-day-old Prince Harry arrived in Kensington Palace for the first time, he was proudly introduced to the family's staff at an informal gathering, before being carried off to the nursery that he would share with his elder brother, William, for the rest of his childhood. As the most important residents of Kensington Palace, the Wales family occupied one of the largest and grandest homes, spanning apartments 8 and 9 on the north side of the palace complex, which incorporates state rooms, offices and several residences put aside for the use of members of the royal family. Charles and Diana had been given the apartment, which was more like a three-storey mansion than a flat, with three reception rooms and three bedroom suites, upon their marriage. Diana had taken a keen interest in its refurbishment, decorating it in soft, pretty pastels and filling it with ornaments and knick-knacks picked up during their travels. Charles's contribution was to borrow antique furniture and paintings from the Royal Collection, including a piano in the drawing room that both boys loved to pretend to play by bashing the keys in imitation of their mother, who was a talented pianist.

The nursery occupied the top floor of the apartment, with bedrooms and bathrooms for the boys and their live-in staff; a kitchen where their simple meals were prepared; an informal dining room; and a sunny, bright-yellow playroom full of colourful toys and books, many of which had been owned by their parents. It was in the cheerful playroom that the boys would spend most of their time, at first just

RIGHT Externally at least, Charles and Diana seemed like the perfect happily married couple. Whatever their differences though, they did their best to provide their sons with a stable and happy childhood in their homes at Kensington Palace and Highgrove

playing but then later on, learning how to read and write before starting school. As Diana had hoped, it was a warm, welcoming and cosy place for the two princes to grow up in and even maintain the illusion of being just a normal pair of little boys, despite the fact that they were living in a palace in the heart of London.

The family's country residence, Highgrove in Wiltshire, was also newly decorated and very comfortable, although it was far more Charles's domain than Diana's, and they would spend rather less time there together – usually only staying at the weekends. At Highgrove, the children, who had their own expansive nursery floor rather like the one at Kensington Palace, were encouraged from an early age to enjoy the country pursuits that the royal family had enjoyed for centuries. It was at Highgrove that the boys kept their beloved Shetland ponies, Smokey and Trigger, and learnt how to ride in the grounds and surrounding lanes. They had their own secluded private garden at Kensington Palace, but it did not offer nearly as much freedom and space

TOP LEFT Charles adored both of his sons, and was an affectionate and involved father, who enjoyed participating in their boisterous games

BOTTOM LEFT Diana created a cosy nursery for the boys at Kensington Palace, full of colourful toys and games. It was an oasis of calm and fun in the otherwise busy palace

as the grounds at Highgrove, where the two boys could happily spend all day running about or playing in their Little Tikes playhouse. They were especially thrilled whenever their father's helicopter landed or took off from Highgrove, and would excitedly clamber inside and explore as soon as the engine was safely switched off.

Both boys were given miniature copies of the 1st Battalion of the Parachute Regiment uniform for Christmas in 1985, complete with matching berets that had been soaked then placed on top of pudding basins in order to shrink them. Typically, William's uniform was for a corporal, while the younger Harry was a lance-corporal – although both were, of course, outranked by their father, who was the regiment's colonel-in-chief.

William was considered to be the 'naughty one' of the pair. Early on, his parents would ruefully comment on his bossiness and total lack of shyness, and describe him as a 'handful'. Insatiably curious, the little boy would wander the palace, always under the watchful eye of his parents or the staff, chatting to anyone whom he encountered, and investigating the apartment's many treasures. Both boys were accustomed from birth to being surrounded by dozens of adults, and as a result, had impeccable manners and a precociously mature outlook and manner of speech.

Their mother, always keen to ensure that their childhoods were as normal as possible, did her best to make sure that they spent as much time as possible with other children, including their numerous cousins on both sides, the offspring of family friends, and the children of their staff, who were welcomed into the family's private quarters to play with the two princes. Particular friends included their cousins Zara and Peter Phillips, the children of Princess Anne; and Princesses Beatrice and Eugenie, the daughters of Prince Andrew, and the royal cousins could often be seen larking around together very happily during the family's regular appearances at official occasions, or on the balcony at Buckingham Palace.

Historically, the relationship between royal siblings, especially when one is the heir and the other the so-called 'spare', has always been a complicated – if not outright hostile – one, but there was never any suggestion of this with these two. From the beginning, William showered his younger brother with affection and attention, and their relationship only grew stronger as the years went by. When Harry learned to walk, it was his elder brother who was at his side, encouraging him on and holding his hand when he faltered, and he would continue to be there for him for all of his milestones. Doubtless they had their squabbles, as all children do, but their parents, who both knew how it felt to be lonely, could at least be satisfied that their children truly cared about each other, and would always have each other. Naturally, Diana adored her boys and they, in turn, loved her very deeply. As her marriage disintegrated, she compensated for this by showering them with the love she felt Charles had rejected, and the three of them became very close. However, Charles was a very involved and affectionate father, himself compensating for his distant relationship with his own parents. Outside their immediate family, both boys would be much loved by their grandparents, the Queen and Duke of Edinburgh, which doubtless did much to heal Prince Charles's complicated feelings about his own childhood.

Diana made sure that life at Kensington Palace and Highgrove was as comfortable and fun as possible for her boys. As she and Charles were often busy with their official duties, the boys spent most of their time with their nanny, 'Baba' Barnes, who supervised their daily routine and acted as a surrogate mother when their real one was absent. When Baba left in 1987, she was replaced by the equally capable Ruth Wallace, with Olga Powell remaining as deputy. Although other nannies would come and go, it was Olga who remained a constant in the princes' lives, a comforting fixture throughout their increasingly turbulent childhood. Although they were showered with presents by both members of the public and foreign dignitaries, and could have had every toy in Harrods if they'd wanted, Diana preferred to keep things simple, and so their toys and activities were ones familiar to almost all British children growing up in the Eighties and Nineties – such as chunky outdoor toys from Little Tikes, wooden rocking horses and jigsaw puzzles. Unlike their father, neither boy was a particularly voracious reader, but it was important to Charles that they be fully prepared for their future duties, and so they were nonetheless expected to learn as much as possible about the world and different cultures, so that they could hold their own in conversations. Ultimately though, both boys much preferred more boisterous play, occasionally with disastrous results. As a toddler, Harry cut his nose while leaping off a table at Highgrove and needed several stitches, while William earned himself the nickname 'Basher', which was much less sweet than his earlier nickname 'Wombat', because of his pugnacity and wilful behaviour. Their grandmother, the Queen, is said to have expressed her dismay at their naughtiness and lack of discipline,

> "It was in the cheerful playroom that the boys would spend most of their time"

BELOW The family's regular annual trips to European skiing resorts were one of the highlights of the princes' calendars, and both would become highly skilled skiers.

WILLIAM | THE HEIR AND THE SPARE

"From the beginning, William showered his younger brother with affection and attention"

but Diana, who knew that they were no worse than any other energetic little boys, refused to intervene – although on occasion, their behaviour was indeed so bad that even she and Charles were driven to sharply reprimand them.

Although at first the boys were rarely seen, as they grew older they began to appear in public more often – usually dressed in matching outfits, which they would later recall with fond mortification, and holding hands with either their mother or their nanny. Charles was keen for them to share his passion for polo, and so early appearances generally took place at Smith's Lawn near Windsor, where the two princes could be seen hanging around the horses or watching their father play from the sidelines. It would be a while before they too were allowed to join in, but in the meantime, they were encouraged to enjoy another family passion – skiing, which involved making an annual trip to Klosters in Switzerland or Lech in Austria every spring. Diana was particularly skilled on the slopes, and to her delight both of her sons turned out to be equally good on skis. Other family holidays included annual trips up to Balmoral in the Scottish Highlands, where they learned to fish and shoot, beach holidays in Majorca or on the Isles of Scilly, and weeks on the Royal Yacht Britannia, where the boisterous pair of little boys would be closely watched at all times lest they decide to jump overboard. Easter every year was spent at Windsor Castle, where they would be given handmade chocolate eggs and sugar mice made by the royal chefs, while Christmas was always spent with the Queen and the rest of the royal family at Sandringham in Norfolk, and followed a strict, traditional programme of presents on Christmas Eve, church on Christmas morning (where they would be expected to dress smartly and be on their very best behaviour), a separate Christmas lunch for the children so the adults could dine in formal splendour,

ABOVE Like most royal children, the princes had riding lessons from a very young age, and quickly became proficient in the saddle

LEFT Prince William and Prince Harry sit together on the steps of Highgrove House wearing army uniforms, having no idea of their future military careers

and – of course – watching their grandmother's annual speech at 3pm along with the rest of the nation.

Their lives were undeniably enormously privileged, and Diana was determined that they should know just how fortunate they were and always be aware of the fact that life for the vast majority of people was not nearly so pleasant. From an early age, both boys occasionally accompanied her to public and private engagements with her charities, particularly those involved with homelessness, addiction and HIV, which served as a stark reminder of just how bleak life can be for those not fortunate enough to be born into royalty. Many other members of the royal family were dismissive of Diana's deep interest in charity work, especially the less photogenic causes that she supported, but she was determined to involve her children from the start, particularly William. Destined to be king one day, Diana felt that he ought to know how his future subjects lived and be able to engage with them. Diana would do her best to keep these visits low key, keen as always to protect her boys from press intrusion. The young princes were often frightened by the large groups of photographers who seemed to lie in wait for them wherever they went, and their mother would do her best to reassure them by saying that they were taking photographs of her and not them. This worked for a while, but as they grew older, the two princes began to find the constant presence of photographers increasingly annoying, and as rumours that their parents' marriage was in trouble continued to multiply, this intrusion, the stress that it caused not just to William and Harry but everyone close to them, and the impact that it would have upon their lives, would only get much worse.

An EDUCATION fit for a KING

William and his brother were the first generation to be educated together in what is to be considered a relatively 'normal' school setting in comparison to previous royal upbringings

In September 1985, Prince William became the first member of the royal family to attend a public nursery when he was enrolled at Mrs Mynors' Nursery School in Notting Hill, London. This was no doubt a decision heavily influenced by Princess Diana, who wanted both her sons to lead as much of an ordinary life as possible. Unfortunately, even this could do little to foster any sense of normality in the young princes' school lives; the press interest in them meant a pack of around 100 journalists awaited William on his very first day, adding to his nerves.

Although it was a public nursery, the fees were still out of reach for many working-class parents, totalling around £780 a year at the time, according to *The Telegraph* – this is the equivalent of £2,200 in today's money. On his very first day, William can be seen leaving the nursery with a finger puppet that he made himself, and the headteacher, Mrs Mynors, said that he enjoyed himself.

By January 1987, William, now aged four, was ready for big school. Wetherby School, an independent pre-preparatory school situated near Kensington Palace, was to be his home for the next few years until just after he turned seven. Here he was popular with his classmates and, having learnt to swim at Buckingham Palace, was awarded a trophy – the Grunfield Cup – for having the best swimming style. He was also said to have had a flair for English and spelling, and he clearly took an active role in school life, performing in Christmas concerts and plays.

RIGHT Diana drops William at Wetherby School in January 1987, aged four. Despite her busy schedule, Diana often made time to do this, ensuring a sense of normality

Both his mum and dad were keen to appear like any other parent, and also took part in the annual sports-day races for parents. However, the next stage of the young prince's educational career would mark a dramatic turning point in his life. No longer would he be in the close vicinity of his mother, who often used to come and pick him up at the end of the day — now he was off to boarding school.

Ludgrove is based in Wokingham, in the heart of the English countryside and roughly 90 minute's drive from the capital. William took his first day in his stride, but his mother was, according to Joann F Price, apparently in tears when she dropped him off there in September 1990. Although he was initially homesick and sent lots of letters home, Price writes in her book, *Prince William: A Biography*, that William would later describe his time at Ludgrove School as some of the "happiest years of his life". Compared to being at Mrs Mynors' and Wetherby, William was shielded from a lot of the intensity from the press.

ABOVE Prince William signs the register of Eton, officially becoming a student, as his father, mother and brother look on

Prince William continued to excel in English, and in 1992 he was awarded the junior essay prize and also had a burgeoning interest in geography. His keen enthusiasm for sport also continued to develop, and it was in the summer of 1991 that he was involved in an accident while playing golf.

According to Andrew Morton's book *Diana: Her True Story*, William received a blow to the head with a golf club in the grounds of Ludgrove from one of his friends after they had been playing together on the putting green. He had to be taken for a CT scan and his mother rushed from her lunch to the school where doctors advised that William should be taken to Great Ormond Street Hospital in an ambulance. The then Prince Charles followed behind in an Aston Martin.

At the hospital, William was operated on for a depressed fracture of the forehead. The accident left him with a lasting wound, which he later described in an interview with cancer patient Alice Marples for the children's BBC programme, *Newsround*, as his Harry Potter scar because he said it sometimes glows.

When it comes to William's later education, it must be seen in the context of his father's schooling. Determined to ensure his children were happier than his allegedly difficult experience at the unconventional Scottish boarding school Gordonstoun, both William and Harry were sent to Eton, Britain's premier public school founded in 1440, which can claim 19 prime ministers and a host of other distinguished public figures to its name.

Eton was to be a new start for Prince William. In his final years at Ludgrove, it had become clear that his parents' marriage was irrevocably breaking down, and he must have been aware of the tension. There was to be no chance of reconciliation and they soon separated. In 1992, Princess Diana had spoken to Andrew Morton for his book, in which she exposed her unhappiness as a member of the royal family. Then, just a few months after William had left Ludgrove, Diana would give her infamous interview to Martin Bashir in which she would claim that Prince Charles had been having a long-term affair with Camilla Parker-Bowles. A formal agreement was struck between Queen Elizabeth's press secretary, Charles Anson, and Lord Wakeham, head of the Press Complaints Commission, that journalists and photographers would leave William in peace to complete his education in exchange for regular updates on his life. Wakeham promised that William would be able to "run, walk, study and play at Eton free from the fear of prying cameras". However, no amount of measures to protect William from the press could have shielded him from the stories about his parents' increasingly acrimonious marriage. It was to this backdrop that Prince William passed the entrance exam to Eton, and in September 1995 – accompanied by his now separated parents and also his younger brother – proudly signed the register, formally admitting himself to the school.

At Eton, William continued to excel at sports. He captained Gailey's team in an inter-house tournament

 *"Around 100 journalists awaited William on his very first day"*

and, according to *The Telegraph*, was befriended by the actor Eddie Redmayne, who said: "...everyone wanted to tackle the future king of England. He took all the hits." William was also good at swimming and was in the top 100 swimmers for his age. Prince William also rose to the top of the school social circle by becoming not just a prefect but also a member of the 'Pop' or the Eton Society, an elite band of prefects that were gifted certain privileges and allowed to sit on the Pop Wall.

Eton also gave William an opportunity to see one of the biggest influences in his life – his grandmother – more often. He apparently regularly went for afternoon tea with her, thanks to Windsor Castle being close to the Eton grounds.

Prince William was keen to follow in his father's footsteps by attending university. But first he had to get the grades. After securing 12 GCSEs, he chose geography, history of art and biology for his A-levels. In terms of his university choice, it has been said he was keen to spread his wings and did not want to attend the traditional establishment institutions of Oxford or Cambridge, his father's alma mater. Instead, he set his sights north of the border to St Andrews in Scotland. Perhaps he was inspired by the Queen's love of Balmoral and the Highlands. Perhaps he was inspired by Scottish devolution and growing Scottish nationalism; after all, the attendance of a future king at a Scottish institution would surely be a symbol that the country wasn't forgotten by the royal family. Or perhaps, like many teenagers applying for university, he simply felt at home there. Nevertheless, in his months at Eton, Prince William worked hard and managed to achieve an A, B and C, more than enough for him to secure his place on the four-year MA in history of art at St Andrews, where the entrance requirements for that year were two Bs and a C.

RIGHT William competes in a sports day at Wetherby School in June 1989 alongside the other students. Here he is about to cross the finishing line in pole position

RIGHT Prince William, photographed at Eton, dons a Union Jack waistcoat to celebrate his 18th birthday. Only members of 'Pop' are allowed to wear waistcoats

PAST-TIMES *of a young* PRINCE

After the separation of Prince Charles and Princess Diana until her death in August 1997, Prince William and Prince Harry would later admit they felt that they were left "bouncing between the two of them"

On 9 December 1992, the world was astounded when the British prime minister, John Major, stood up in the House of Commons and announced that the then Prince and Princess of Wales had decided to separate, adding that it was amicable, they had no plans to divorce (although they later did) and that there was every chance that Diana might still be crowned queen one day. There had been rumours that the Waleses' marriage was on the rocks for nearly a decade, but even so, this stark, official announcement took almost everyone by surprise. While the country and international press dissected this unexpected turn of events, and speculated about what precisely had gone wrong between the royal couple, Charles and Diana were, like all newly separated couples, privately working out the minutiae of their new lives – in particular the arrangements for their beloved boys. It was immediately announced that while Charles would now be dividing his time between Highgrove and Clarence House, Diana would be remaining in their apartment in Kensington Palace, and that the boys would be dividing their time between them when they weren't at school, with both parents equally responsible for their upbringing.

Ten-year-old William and eight-year-old Harry had been aware for quite some time that their parents' marriage was failing – it would have been impossible not to notice the growing air of tension between Charles and Diana as they led increasingly separate lives and spent as little time as possible in each other's company. Even so, the news of their separation, which was gently broken to them in private, hit them both very hard.

The royal family, in particular their grandparents, Queen Elizabeth II and Prince Philip, now rallied around to make sure that they felt fully loved and supported at this difficult time, which was made all the more onerous by all of the public attention now trained upon them.

In some ways, though, it must have been a relief – their mother was often miserable and in tears, and would even later on recall her eldest son passing tissues to her under a bathroom door and begging her not to cry as she sobbed helplessly on the other side. After the separation, both parents became visibly happier, and as a consequence the princes, too, felt the mood lighten at home. Despite this, it was tough to go to school knowing that their classmates and teachers knew all about their parents' private affairs. In particular, for William, the sensitive and reserved elder boy who

RIGHT As young men, Prince William and Prince Harry's pastimes were determined by their parents, Charles and Diana. Each had their own ideas about what the young boys needed to blow off steam from their upcoming royal duties

already deeply resented the relentless press intrusion into their lives, it was especially painful.

Although tensions were high between the adults of the royal family during the separation of Charles and Diana, princes William and Harry, who were ten and eight years old respectively at the time of the split in December 1992, gained some distance from the drama while attending independent boarding school Ludgrove in the heart of rural Berkshire. While it was a disruptive time in their lives, the boys were provided with ample opportunities for fun and entertainment by their peers and parents. Now that they spent time with their mother and father separately, the arguments and frustrations that had spoilt family events in the past were no more.

William and Harry spent their first Christmas following the news of their parents' split at Sandringham House with their father and grandmother, the late queen. The Boxing Day pheasant shoot at the 20,000-acre Norfolk estate is one of the biggest events of the year to be held by the royal family, and both boys were encouraged to get on board with the tradition from an early age. One such activity undertaken by the young princes was hunting, although their mother greatly disapproved. Regardless, both were taught to respect guns, and as soon as they were old enough, they were allowed to attend the Boxing Day hunt organised by their father.

William had been watching the shoot from the age of just four and was an impressive shot, even as a child. Also a keen supporter of traditional activities, Charles would ensure that both boys were active participants in hunting, hiking and fishing, taking them on trips and days out to better their skills. However, it wasn't just about teaching the boys — it was also a chance to bond with them at such a difficult time.

William enjoyed acting, starring in Ludgrove School's Christmas plays

LEFT Family has always been important to William and Harry, and they would attend lots of family events as children. Even as youngsters, they had a close relationship with their grandmother and great grandmother

year after year. He also became the secretary of acting for Ludgrove's Dramatic Society, embracing his role as a leader. In March 1993, his parents watched him parade on stage again as he played Napoleon in John Harris' play *The Sword of General Frapp*. At Ludgrove, Harry also participated in drama, taking part in the school's production of The Lion, the Witch and the Wardrobe during his final year.

As a woman who had married into royalty, Diana was insistent that the boys have as 'normal' a life as possible, although this wasn't always feasible for members of one of the most watched and admired families in the world. With their mother and father dominating the tabloids with their marital problems, it was even more difficult at times — but it didn't stop

 *"They engaged in water fights and played outside with their friends"*

the youngsters from having fun like ordinary children.

Under the terms of the separation, Diana had custody of the boys on alternate weekends and agreed holidays. In London, she made sure that life for her sons was comfortable and fun, allowing them to watch television and rent videos they could watch together, like *Rambo*. The boys also got to indulge in computer games.

Time with their mother didn't stop her busy schedule, but she did involve the boys in her plans, taking them to the gym with her, where they played tennis. Years of lessons meant they grew into accomplished players. Conversely, the brothers often stayed at home, riding their bikes around Kensington Palace's vast grounds. Still only children, they engaged in summer

water fights and played outside with their friends.

The young princes were exposed to a number of different experiences thanks to the princess. She took them to the cinema, book store WHSmith, McDonalds, to see Father Christmas at Selfridges, and on public transport.

The two children often enjoyed visits to a Berkshire go-karting circuit and were also treated to days out to watch the Grand Prix. In the summer of 1993, the paparazzi, desperate to catch glimpses of a post-princess Diana, snapped pictures of the princes and their mother at the Silverstone Circuit enjoying a day out.

When spending time with their father, the boys were usually under the supervision of 28-year-old Tiggy Legge-Bourke, and they grew to adore her, looking up to her as essentially a cool older sister. She had been an assistant to Charles' private secretary, becoming a nanny after the Prince of Wales' separation from Diana.

RIGHT When spending time with their father, the princes often spent time with their nanny, Tiggy Legge-Bourke. Diana was not always impressed with the nanny's mannerisms but the boys adored their companion

Although excited to join in with whatever plans his parents had for him and his brother, William tended to be most interested in horse riding and shooting in his free time. The princes also learned to play polo, riding different kinds of horses, practising with sticks and starting off by playing bicycle polo with other children before progressing to the real thing, always improving as they grew up.

By 1995, relations had further soured between Charles and Diana, and the boys continued to divide their time between both parents who, unbeknown to the public, were fast approaching an official divorce. That summer, William, keen to try every sport, took part in Ludgrove's father-and-son clay pigeon shooting competition with Charles, which the pair won.

One of the happiest times during that summer for the brothers came in July — the Everton versus Manchester United match in the FA Cup Final. The princes were allowed the afternoon off school to attend with their father. Sitting in the Royal Box at Wembley Stadium, 13-year-old William and 11-year-old Harry cheered wildly although officially they held no allegiance to either team.

In July 1995, Diana and William played in the mother-and-son tennis competition at Ludgrove School and, although they didn't win, it was evident that they had enjoyed the experience together.

During the final years of Diana's life, the boys continued to enjoy themselves, venturing on wild adventures with both parents — including a trip to Balmoral with their father just weeks before the tragic death of Diana in August 1997 at the age of 36. The boys were just 15 and 12.

Yet undeterred by the strains of their family life, throughout their childhoods the young princes were always pictured with huge grins, much to their parents' delight.

Images: Getty

Both young princes followed in their father's footsteps as keen polo players, learning the sport on bicycles first before progressing to the fast-paced challenge of horseback

ROYAL TRIPS and HOLIDAYS

As a young man, Prince William would do much more than build his life around his royal titles. Both his mother and father wanted him and Prince Harry to experience everything that life had to offer, with family holidays providing experiences to shape his later life

William and Harry spent the first Christmas after their parents separated in late 1992 with their father at Sandringham Palace, while their mother saw her own circle of friends and family. But with the festivities over and the New Year just around the corner, Diana whisked her young sons off to the tropical island of Nevis in the Caribbean in the company of Diana's friends and their children for some quality time together. The party stayed at the Montpelier Plantation & Beach, a charming and luxurious location on an old sugar plantation covering 60 acres and comprising private chalets. Armed with a packed lunch made by the hotel staff, William and Harry rode in pick-up trucks and visited beaches like the Indian Castle Beach or Pinney's Beach, where they would enjoy a picnic and an afternoon of bodyboarding and jumping off the back of a speed boat into the clear waters. As mischievous as ever, the young Prince Harry also organised the 'Nevis Toad Derby', collecting as many as a dozen giant cane toads from the island and lining them up for a course, selecting the "most streamlined, athletic-looking toads for themselves," according to the former bodyguard of Diana, Ken Wharfe. The rest of the party were then instructed to pick their competitors in the race. Unfortunately for everyone, each toad hopped off in a different direction, but for the boys, the dawning of 1993 brought with it the possibility of more adventures in a slightly happier – if not, ever so slightly more dysfunctional – family unit.

Holidays were a wonderful time for William. Prior to his parents' split, the well-enjoyed trips fell under strain with his parents growing more acrimonious towards one another. The last ski trip that William and Harry ever had with both of their parents was to the Austrian slopes of Lech in March 1992. The trip was cut short when Diana's father, the 8th Earl Edward John 'Johnnie' Spencer, died of a heart attack just a few days before the trip was to end. Diana and Charles rushed home, while the boys continued their holiday with the rest of the party, which was made up of some of Diana's friends, as well as friends of William and Harry, the boys' nanny and protection officers. But in the aftermath of the split, Princess Diana had wanted to maintain a stable life for the boys, and so in March

RIGHT Holidays allowed Prince William and Harry to escape the media onslaught of their parents' split. Trips to Thorpe Park provided endless hours of entertainment, which their mother insisted they enjoy alongside everyone else, refusing special treatment

1993, a year after the last visit to the slopes, the boys returned with their mother and, as always, stayed in the Arlberg Hotel. Skiing was not the only snow sport that William enjoyed during these trips to the mountains – the party was papped sleigh-riding around the town with their nanny, Olga Powell, and a protection officer. The group would return to Lech many more times, including the following year with Diana's friends, Kate Menzies and Catherine Soames.

But holidays and trips weren't all about the overseas adventures. Having visited Britain's biggest theme park, Thorpe Park, in the spring of 1992, the young princes were spotted returning once again in 1993, enjoying the daring and thrilling rides offered at the park with their mother. Diana was insistent that they wait in line for the rides like everyone else, refusing royal treatment. During their 1993 visit, a film crew were invited to follow the royals around the park. William and Harry were photographed on the Loggers Leap, with their mother laughing wildly beside them. Video footage captured the brothers enjoying rides such as the Teacup Ride, Thunder River, Depth Charge and the Hudson River Rafters accompanied by Colin Dawson, the general manager of Thorpe Park at the time.

In the summer of 1993, William and Harry ventured to Cornwall without either of their parents – the first holiday they had without them. In the wake of the 'Squidgygate' scandal, and in turn the 'Camillagate' scandal – which were recorded illicit phone calls between either parent to their secret paramours – both boys were under unimaginable pressure to avoid the racy and intrusive headlines on either parent. Finding some solace at Polzeath in Cornwall with their good friends, the van Straubenzee boys, whose parents rented the same clifftop house there every year, William got to experience a small amount of time as regular child, playing outside with his friends in the baking summer sun.

BELOW Austria's city of Lech was a guaranteed good time for the princes, who would visit year after year with their mother

Diana loved to take the boys on fun holidays, and in August 1993 William and Harry stayed at Disney World's Grand Floridian Resort and Spa for three days, where they had the run of the entire fifth floor, which their mother had rented out. At the resort's Magic Kingdom, a private escort helped to navigate the party through the theme park's best rides, secretly whisking them through underground tunnels, although it is highly doubtful that the boys needed any encouragement to board the vast array of exciting rides available at the resort. The paparazzi snapped a picture of the princes aboard a log flume, screaming as their flume slid over the intense drop. While at the park they also boarded rides like the Country Bear Jamboree, the Jungle Cruise and Big Thunder Mountain Railroad.

> "In the aftermath of the split, Diana wanted to maintain a stable life for the boys"

The young princes also enjoyed trips with their father, despite the British tabloids dissecting every part of the royal split and running headlines that suggested Charles was an absent parent. After returning from their 1993 skiing trip with Diana, William and Harry were whisked off on a cruise to the Greek Islands on board MV Alexander with their father. In 1994 and the subsequent years after, William and his brother indulged in some father-and-sons time in the Switzerland slopes of Klosters.

William and Harry also spent plenty of time at Balmoral Castle in Scotland with their father, hiking, hunting and fishing – it was a somewhat home away from home for the young boys, and the place they would be when they learned of their mother's tragic car crash a few years later.

While Diana was all about her sons having fun, she also wanted them to learn about humility and to be active in helping those less fortunate. In 1994, before either boy had reached their teenage years, their mother took them to The Passage homeless shelter. Diana was adamant that, unlike Charles and the rest of the royals, William and Harry would both grow up being aware of what life was like away from the royal bubble. As both boys have grown into men and started their own families, they have frequented some of the projects founded and directed by their mother, and spent time at not only homeless shelters, but children's hospitals, drug rehabilitation centres and residencies for the mentally handicapped across the globe.

By 1996, Charles and Diana's divorce was official. The last holiday William would ever get with his mother was in July 1997, venturing to the French Riviera in Saint Tropez. Prince Harry's 12th birthday was just around the corner when he and William stayed at the heavily guarded luxury villa of Egyptian businessman and billionaire Mohamed Al-Fayed, whose son – Dodi Fayed – was their mother's current love interest. While holidaying in the French Riviera, the boys rode speed boats, dashing across the waters like young James Bonds, and swam in the crystal-blue waters. During this holiday, they boarded the Fayed family's multi-million-dollar yacht, Jonikal, in the Mediterranean sea. Swimming in the sun-drenched waters off Sardinia's Emerald Coast, William was unaware that these tranquil moments in his mother's company were to be the final ones he would experience with her. After enjoying themselves in the sun, the young princes returned to the UK and headed off to Balmoral for some quality time with their father and grandmother. They had been due to reunite with their mother in August, but while at Balmoral, the news of his mother's death was a tsunami that changed William's life forever.

TOP RIGHT On the tropical island of Nevis, William made frequent trips to Indian Castle Beach with his family, playing in the clear waters

MIDDLE RIGHT William's father was more of a traditionalist when it came to holidays, favouring sporting activities such as skiing in the Swiss peaks

RIGHT Pictures of Princess Diana and her sons at Thorpe Park showed the family deliriously happy to be enjoying quality time together in the wake of such a tough time for the royal family

Images: Getty

The DEATH of DIANA

The tragic and untimely death of the late Princess of Wales had a profound effect upon her sons, as well as the world

On 31 August 1997, the country woke up to the shocking news that Diana, Princess of Wales, had died in Paris just hours earlier. Within half an hour of the news breaking, the first bouquet had been placed outside the gates of Kensington Palace – the first of thousands that would arrive over the following days as the public, most of whom had never even met Diana, sought to express their grief and total disbelief that she was gone, and that the story that had begun with a fairy-tale wedding 16 years earlier had now met such a tragic end.

After her divorce was finalised a year earlier in August 1996, Diana had worked extremely hard to find her feet. Her tempestuous two-year relationship with cardiologist Hasnat Khan had finally come to an end in June 1997, and shortly afterwards she had frequently been seen in the company of Dodi Fayed, the playboy son of Harrods owner Mohamed Al-Fayed, whom she had met while staying at his father's villa in St Tropez with her sons at the start of July. At the end of the month, William and Harry had joined their father at Balmoral, but they were planning to rejoin their mother on the last day of August before returning to Eton.

At the end of August, Dodi and Diana enjoyed a break in Sardinia on his father's yacht before going to Paris, where they planned to stay in the Fayed-owned Ritz Hotel on the Place Vendôme. However, the pair decided to retreat from the Ritz, where it seemed like every press photographer in Paris was lying in wait for them, and instead stay at Dodi's father's apartment near the Champs-Élysées.

They set off at 12.20am in the back of a black Mercedes, which was driven by the Ritz deputy head of security, Henri Paul, with bodyguard Trevor Rees-Jones sitting in the passenger seat. Neither Diana nor Dodi were wearing a seat belt, while Paul had spent the evening drinking alcohol

RIGHT Diana blossomed after the divorce, and threw herself into her new role as ambassadress for her favourite causes, such as the removal of landmines in Angola

in the bar and would later prove to be over the legal driving limit. Diana would never have been allowed to travel in such unsafe conditions in the past, but when she lost her right to be addressed as 'Your Royal Highness' she also gave up her right to a royal security team, who would have prevented her from getting into Dodi's car that fateful evening.

Pursued by a swarm of photographers, the Mercedes sped away from the Ritz, crossed the Place de la Concorde and headed towards the Champs-Élysées. Disaster soon struck after they entered the underpass tunnel by the Pont de l'Alma as Henri Paul lost control of the speeding Mercedes and crashed it into one of the many pillars that lined the tunnel.

When the first of the pursuing paparazzi arrived at the scene just a few moments later, they were horrified to discover that the Mercedes was now a mangled mess of metal, and that the driver and Dodi Fayed were clearly dead, while bodyguard Rees-Jones had severe injuries to his face. Most attention, however, was on the injured but still conscious Diana, who was crumpled in the back of the vehicle. As they waited for emergency services to arrive, some of the photographers tried to help, but others continued to take

Image: Getty

LEFT The funeral of Diana, Princess of Wales, was watched by more than a million people on the streets, more than 31 million on television in the UK, and around two billion worldwide. For her sons and family it was still an intensely personal event, made all the more difficult by the knowledge that the eyes of the world were on them

LEFT Prince Charles holds the hand of Prince Harry as they view bouquets of flowers left in memory of Diana, Princess of Wales, in September 1997 in Balmoral, Scotland

photographs despite entreaties to stop.

Although it had at first seemed possible that she might survive the catastrophe, once Diana was released from the wreckage it became clear just how serious her injuries were. She suffered a cardiac arrest and required ten minutes of CPR before she was considered stable enough to be moved. Despite the best efforts of French medical staff at the Pitié-Salpêtrière Hospital in Paris, Diana was declared dead at 4am local time.

Several hundred miles away at Balmoral Castle, it was just 3am, and the two princes were fast asleep after a busy day playing with their cousins. They had not seen their mother for almost a month but had kept in regular contact, her last brief call having been made from Paris the previous evening. Much later, the two boys would recall cutting the phone call short because they wanted to return to the game they were playing, and regretted not having spoken to her for much longer.

Their father was informed of the accident at 1am, and had anxiously waited for news until confirmation arrived that Diana had died in hospital. Devastated, he spent the next few hours walking around the gardens and worrying about how to tell his children that their mother was dead, before finally waking William just after 7am. Afterwards, he went to Harry's room to break the news. Later that Sunday morning, the trio, obviously completely stunned and suffering terribly, accompanied the rest of the royal family to morning service at the local church. There was no mention of Diana during the service, which prompted the young Harry to ask his father if his mother was really dead. When Charles made arrangements to travel to Paris in order to bring Diana's body back to London, Harry begged to accompany him but was gently advised to remain with his grandparents.

Although everyone was deeply shocked and distressed by Diana's sudden death, the chief priority of everyone at Balmoral was to ensure

ABOVE The images of the young princes following Diana's coffin shocked and moved the public, and remain an enduring testament to the love they had for their mother

that her two anguished sons received as much support as possible. Their often-irascible grandfather, Prince Philip, was especially supportive of them at this time. He had not been much older than William when he experienced the tragedy of losing his favourite sister, Cecilie, along with her husband and three of their children in a plane crash, and so had a better idea than most of how they may be feeling.

He took them on several long hikes and stalks through the estate at this time, allowing them to either walk in silence or talk about their feelings. Meanwhile, their grandmother, the Queen, ordered that all newspapers be banned from the castle, and that every television and radio be hidden away in order to protect them from the round-the-clock coverage and the lurid speculations and sensationalism being spread by the press.

Their aunt, Princess Anne, who admittedly had never been very fond of Diana but loved her boys, was also extremely supportive, particularly of Harry, who was clearly struggling and whom she took out on long rides. She also enlisted her children, Zara and Peter, to take the lost, anguished boys under their wings.

However, as the royal family firmly closed ranks to protect and care for the two boys at the very heart of this terrible tragedy, it began to look to the public as though they were actively shunning the huge outpouring of collective grief that had greeted the news of Diana's passing.

Some royal deaths, notably that of the Queen's own father, George VI, had been marked by genuine mourning on the part of the public, but the establishment had never before seen anything on such an enormous scale, and so they underestimated just how seriously the public mourning should be taken and miscalculated their response to it. The late Queen and Prince Philip were so focused on protecting William and Harry from the spotlight and treating the death of their mother as a private tragedy that they failed to appreciate the feelings of a nation that also felt bereaved.

Only Charles seemed to understand, and he was the driving force behind the family's acknowledgement of Diana's popularity and status. It was he who insisted upon a public funeral at Westminster Abbey when his parents were instead in favour of the Spencer family organising a private ceremony.

Family discussions about the funeral naturally involved some discussion of the role that the two princes should play, and at one point an enraged Prince Philip burst out, "Stop telling us what to do with those boys! They've lost their mother and you're talking about them as though they're commodities! Have you any idea what they're going through?" At another time, he interrupted a discussion to say that the most pressing matter on his mind was the fact that William had run away somewhere on the Balmoral estate and couldn't be found.

Meanwhile, the press continued to condemn the royal family's lack of visibility, which prompted the late Queen's press secretary to remind them that although "the princess was a much-loved national figure... she was also a mother whose sons miss her deeply. Prince William and Prince Harry themselves want to be with their father and their grandparents at this time in the quiet haven of Balmoral."

The princes returned to London with their father on 5 September, the day before their mother's funeral. Her body was still lying in the chapel at St James's Palace, and they privately went there that evening to view her, the coffin having been specially lowered so that they would be able to see her face for the last time.

The following morning, to the surprise of many, they joined the funeral procession when it moved past St James's Palace and, along with their father, grandfather and uncle, Earl Spencer, proceeded to walk behind the coffin as it slowly made its way to Westminster Abbey.

Debate had privately raged for days about whether the boys should walk in the procession, with William being particularly unwilling to expose his private grief to the crowds that would be gathered for the occasion, but when Prince Philip offered to walk with him, he gave in, much later admitting in an interview that he was glad to have done so, although at the time he was bewildered by the overwhelming public reaction to his mother's death, and tried to hide his face behind his hair as he walked.

Harry has also stated that he too is now glad that he took part, having previously struggled with the ordeal, once candidly revealing: "I don't think any child should be asked to do that, under any circumstances."

During the walk, which was often punctuated by the anguished screams and cries of the crowds, the visibly devastated but dignified boys were kept distracted by their grandfather, Prince Philip, who chatted to them and pointed out the various London landmarks that they were passing.

Later that day they were able to escape the crowds and say a far more private farewell to their mother when her body was finally laid to rest on an island at the Spencer family home in Althorp where she had grown up.

For the public, the death and funeral of Diana, Princess of Wales, marked the terrible and dramatic end of what had been – in more ways than one – a fairy tale. However, for her two grieving boys, William and Harry, it was the beginning of a long and devastating struggle to cope with the crushing loss of an adored parent.

While the press and public continued to have an immense interest in Diana's life and death – right up to this day – William and Harry did not speak publically about her passing and how it affected them until the 20th anniversary of her death approached in 2017. In the HBO documentary *Diana, Our Mother*, the pair reflected on their relationship with their mother, with William warmly remembering that "she was very informal and really enjoyed laughter and fun."

William also opened up in an honest interview with journalist Alastair Campell for the July issue of British *GQ* that year. Discussing what it was like to lose his mother at such a young age, he admitted that walking behind her coffin "was one of the hardest things I have ever done" and that he struggled to grieve properly for many years. However, he also revealed that he was "in a better place about it", stating that "it has taken me almost 20 years to get to that stage. I still find it difficult now because at the time it was so raw. And also it is not like most people's grief, because everyone else knows about it, everyone knows the story, everyone knows her."

While William spoke about Diana's death, he also took the opportunity to

ABOVE After returning to London, the princes and their father took the time to survey the sea of flowers that had surrounded Kensington Palace since Diana's death

discuss his feelings about the media and its role in her tragic passing. "This was a young woman with a high profile position, very vulnerable, desperate to protect herself and her children...I feel very sad and I still feel very angry that we were not old enough to be able to do more to protect her, not wise enough to step in and do something that could have made things better for her. I hold a lot of people to account that they did not do what they should have done, out of human decency."

The impact of the press on Diana's life was brought into the spotlight once again in 2020, when it was revealed that the princess had

> *"'Stop telling us what to do with those boys! You're talking like they're commodities!'"*

been deceived by journalist Martin Bashir into giving her infamous 1995 *Panorama* interview. Bashir had shown her brother, Earl Spencer, fake bank statements that indicated people close to Diana were being paid to spy on her. Having gained Spencer's trust, Bashir was then introduced to Diana and he persuaded her to agree to an interview, allegedly using false allegations about the royal family to convince her. An independent inquiry in 2021 found that Bashir had acted in a "deceitful" way and that the BBC's own internal inquiry into the matter, held in 1996, was "woefully ineffective."

After the inquiry's findings were announced, William issued a statement condemning the BBC, stating that "The deceitful way the interview was obtained substantially influenced what my mother said." He said the interview had contributed to her "fear, paranoia and isolation" and had made his parents' relationship worse, and that "it is my firm view that this *Panorama* programme holds no legitimacy and should never be aired again."

Even though the last few years of Diana's life were difficult in many ways, it is clear that she adored her sons and tried to bring love, fun and enjoyment into their lives as much as possible. And, as the Prince of Wales' reflections in recent years have shown, Diana's love and warmth have left a lasting impact on him and his brother.

RAISED *in the* SPOTLIGHT

No other royal has experienced such intensive press attention from such an early age as Prince William and his brother. William's very first hours were photographed and his early years were filled with photo calls but as he grew up, the pitfalls of such press attention became tragically real

The media has been a major part of Prince William's life from the moment he was born, and even in his darkest hour he couldn't escape it. The death of Diana on 31 August 1997 dominated TV, radio, newspapers and magazines around the world, and her sons were as much a part of the story as Diana herself. Just hours after learning of their loss, William and Harry were photographed on their way to church at Crathie near Balmoral, where they were staying with their father. Media gathered round the tiny kirk as the boys, pale and clearly in shock, went to a Sunday morning service with their family. William turned his head away, Harry stared straight in front, and the images were seen across the globe. But while millions turned to the media for news of the lost princess and her grieving sons, just as many were blaming parts of it for her death.

The royal family tried to shield William and Harry from the media coverage in the hours and days after Diana's death. But journalists focused on the paparazzi that had surrounded Diana's car in the Alma tunnel in Paris in the moments before the crash, along with the stories that some had taken pictures of her as she lay injured in the wreckage. Even after a French judicial investigation in 1999 concluded the crash had been caused by the driver being under the influence of drink and prescription drugs, the animosity towards

RIGHT No part of William's childhood escaped press attention; even a bike ride with his dad and brother at Sandringham

the media remained. By the time a 2008 British inquest into the death placed the blame with the driver and the paparazzi pursuing her car, anger towards the media had dimmed. But in September 1997, as the world focused on the role the media played in Diana's death, her sons were given a very real reminder of how big a role the press played in royal life.

Ensuring that William and Harry didn't see the almost blanket coverage of their mother's death and the huge outpouring of grief that followed was a major operation. In the few short hours between learning of his ex-wife's passing and waking his sons to tell them, Charles had TVs and radios removed from the boys' bedrooms to keep the news from them.

In the following days, newspapers were also hidden – no one wanted them to see the graphic images of the car in which their mother had been travelling, or read the coverage of the anger being expressed by some that the royal family was acting coldly and ignoring the grief of the country. The priority at Balmoral was to protect and support William and Harry.

> *"The priority was to protect William & Harry"*

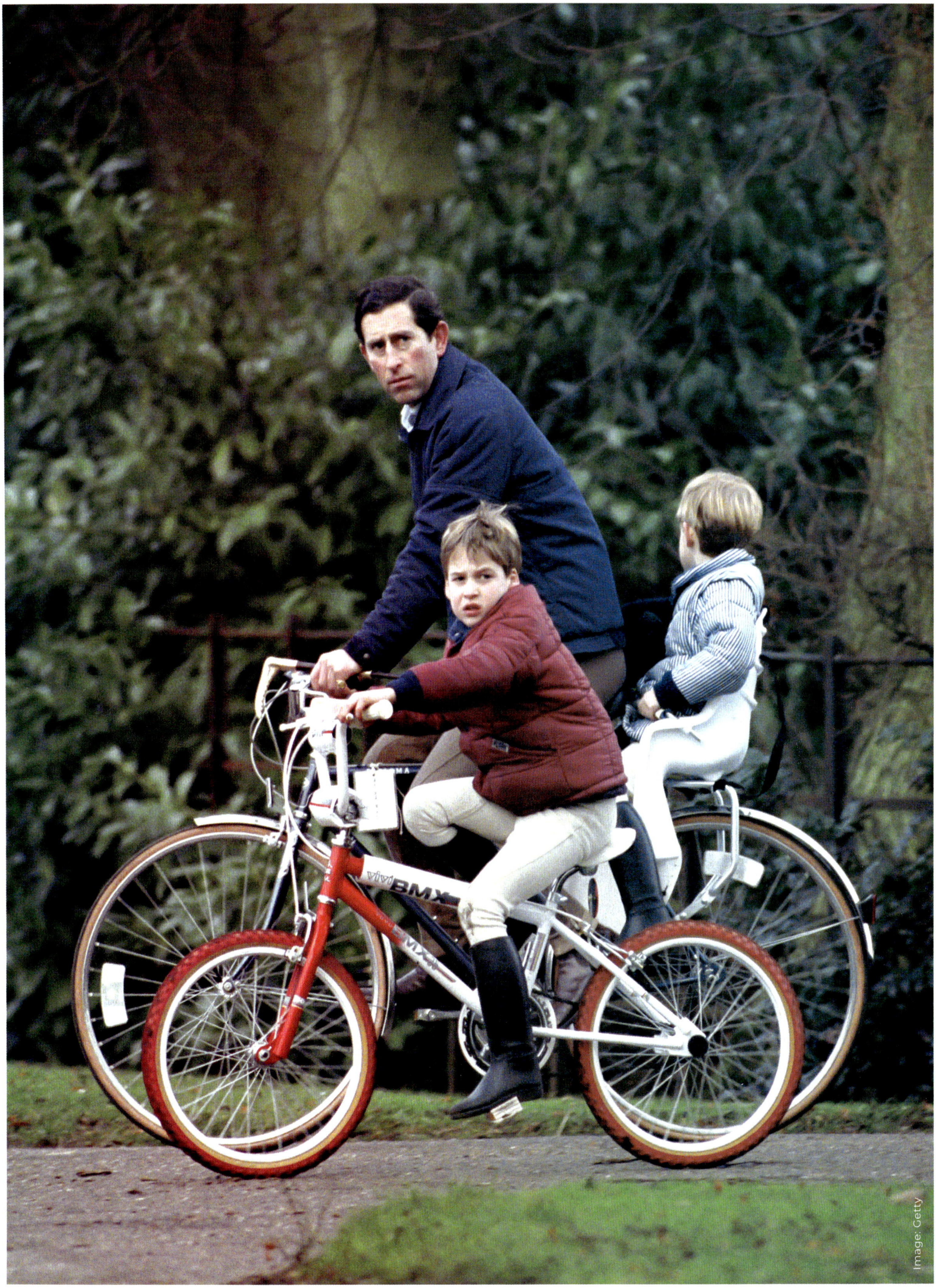

Image: Getty

But in the days before the funeral, they themselves became the focal point of media attention as they appeared in public, at Balmoral and in London, to see some of the many tributes left to Diana while cameras clicked and reporters made notes. A deal was struck between the palace and the press not to show the princes' tears during Diana's funeral, but that didn't stop William and Harry being acutely aware that their grief was a story being covered around the world as they walked behind the coffin.

The princes had both been brought up knowing that the press would be a major part of their lives. While they had slept happily through their first media moments as they were carried out of hospital by their parents before banks of photographers, their awareness of the press developed from their early days. Prince William first met the media en masse at the age of ten months when he was snapped playing with his parents in the grounds of Government House in Auckland while on their tour of New Zealand. By the time he carried out another photo call, just before Harry's birth in 1984, he was so used to seeing the press that he marched up to a TV camera demanding to know more. Similar arranged media moments occurred with regularity for both princes, and in their early days they appeared to breeze through them.

But William and Harry learned early on that they couldn't cherry-pick when they met the media. From their very first appearances at big, royal events like Trooping the Colour, they were aware of the cameras being trained

BELOW Clearly at ease posing for the cameras, Prince William engages with the press on his second birthday at Kensington Palace

> "*The royal family tried to shield William and Harry from the media coverage*"

on them. Both boys also faced major moments in their lives in front of the press. Around 100 photographers were waiting for three-year-old Prince William when he started Mrs Mynors' Nursery School in 1985. William and Harry would also find the press waiting for them at all the major moments of their academic lives, as their parents agreed to coverage of events like their first days and Christmas plays if the princes were left alone the rest of the time.

Other situations weren't so easy to control. Ordinary childhood moments, like William being told off by Diana at a polo match, were splashed across the world's newspapers, and the boys became increasingly aware of the cameras surrounding them whenever they stepped outdoors. In the early 1990s, they both witnessed their mother becoming frustrated with photographers trying to snap the family on holiday outside of the agreed press calls that were designed to offer some privacy.

William, speaking years later, recalled seeing his mother taunted by photographers trying to get a picture of her. While their parents had tried their best to make media interest in them normal and, to a degree, manageable, the downside of tabloid press interest was clear for William to see from an early age.

The princes were also increasingly aware of the media focus on their parents' marital woes. With both Charles and Diana deciding to co-operate on various books and TV interviews, they knew their family split was being read and discussed around the world and it took its toll. In the summer of 1997, William asked both his parents to stay away from his sports day at Eton because he was worried about the media interest and its impact on his friends.

Even before his mother's death, William had become more wary of the press. On their last holiday together, Diana had remonstrated with media trying to snap her and her boys from a helicopter, saying William was "freaked out" by it. The last time the boys were seen in public before Diana's death was at Balmoral where they posed for photographers alongside their father. But nothing could have prepared them for the interest after their mother's death. In the four weeks following the crash, nearly 40 percent of all British newspaper copy was linked to Diana and her sons. As they returned to school, the story of their mother's death continued to be told in the media. It was a constant reminder of how big a part the press had played in Diana's royal role and the impact it would continue to have on both princes for the rest of their lives.

RIGHT Prince William grew up around the press, but as he grew older, the intrusion into his life became harder to deal with

"The downside of tabloid press interest was clear for William to see from an early age"

PRINCE WILLIAM at UNIVERSITY

Prince William followed in his father's footsteps by pursuing a university education, and earned himself a place as one of the royal family's 'brainiest' members. But from the start, he made it clear that he wanted to do it his way, based on merit alone and not on his status. For four years, William got to experience a period of relative peace away from the constant attention of the press. During this time, he finally got the chance to be considered 'ordinary', settling in to the everyday life of a student

When Prince William announced that his first choice for university was St Andrews, Scotland, it came as a surprise. Royals had traditionally attended either Oxford or Cambridge, and many were expecting William to choose the latter as his father had earned his own university degree there during the early Seventies. But William, whose education had routinely broken with royal tradition from the start, decided to go somewhere different.

The Prince admitted that his desire to attend St Andrews was driven by the fact that he "wanted to get away and try somewhere else". Obviously, he had lived in England and knew that one day, as the heir apparent to the throne, he would make frequent visits to Scotland. St Andrews, a rather remote town on the east coast of Fife, suited him better than the hectic and busy lifestyle at Edinburgh University. His bodyguards were supposedly very glad about William's choice, aware that it would be far easier for them to protect him in a quieter place.

As soon as William's choice had been made public, the 'Prince William effect' took hold of the university. It became inundated with applications, which had rocketed by 44 percent compared to the previous year. The desire to attend

RIGHT William with his father on his first day at university – just like any other parent and child, you can see the nerves bubbling under the surface

the same institution as William meant there were around 9,212 people fighting for one of the 1,250 places available. Despite the furor surrounding William, he remained positive that he would be able to live the life of an ordinary student. He stated that the heightened attention would "get easier as time goes on," as the novelty of his status would eventually wear off.

As the oldest university in Scotland, first founded in 1413, St Andrews University has a long history. However, William was not the first royal to attend St Andrews, as King James II of Scotland had done so during the 15th century. William was reportedly determined to succeed on his merit and grades alone, working hard to achieve an A, a B and a C in his A-levels. After his gap year, William moved to Scotland to begin his four-year degree in history of art in September 2001. Before the start of the

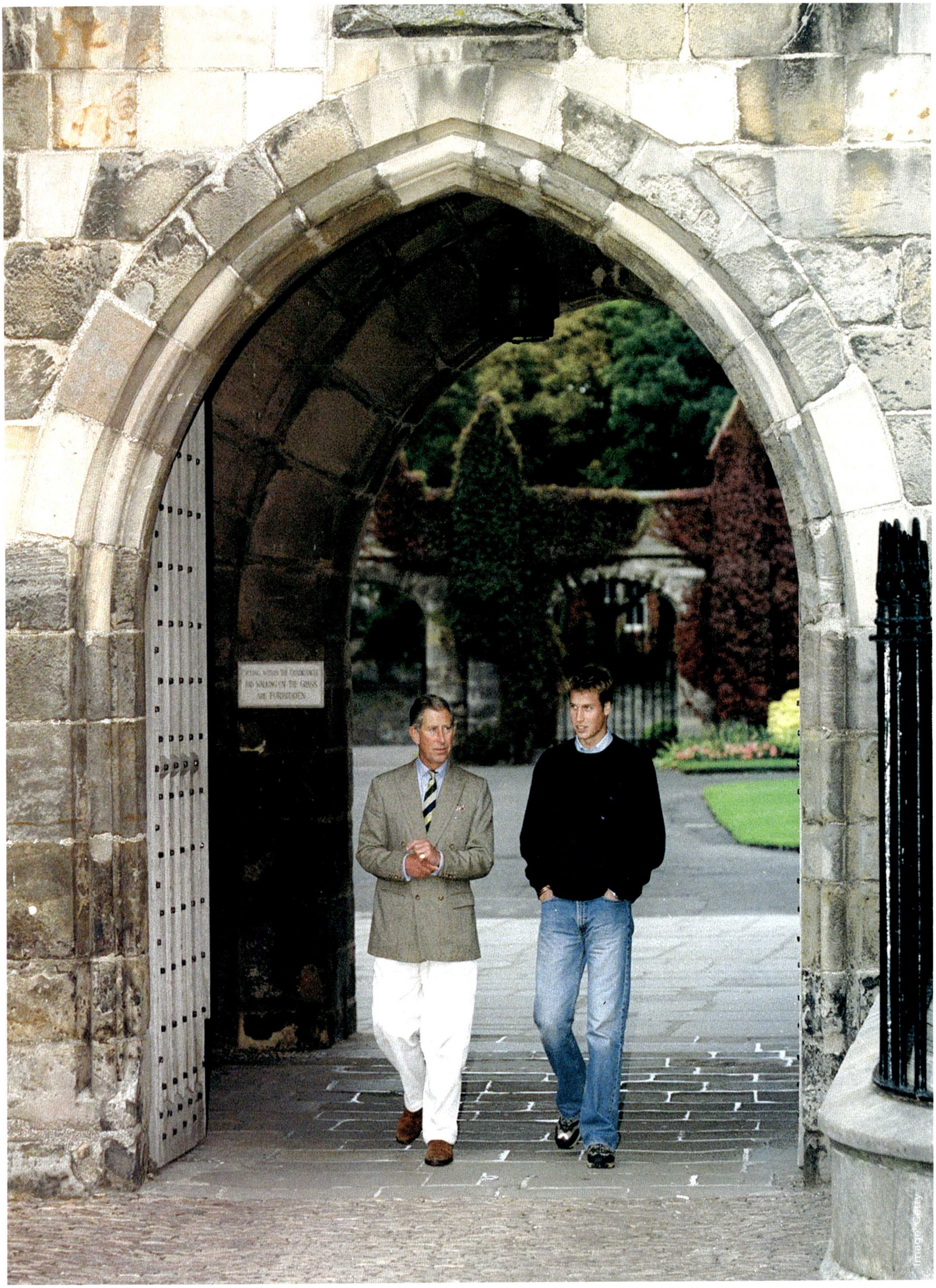

Image: Getty

academic term, it was announced that the Prince would not be taking part in freshers' week.

The British press had quietly agreed throughout the education of both Prince William and Prince Harry to leave them alone, which continued during William's time at St Andrews. As a thank you, William joined his father for day visits in Paisley, Glasgow and Edinburgh, many of them in connection with the charitable activities of the Prince's Trust. On 24 September, William arrived to begin his studies at St Andrews to a crowd of 2,000 people, quickly disappearing into his accommodation. There were a few interview and photo-call opportunities for the press during William's time at university but for the most part, he was left to enjoy university as an ordinary student.

Nonetheless, a minor scandal broke out when it had emerged that a television company, Ardent Productions, had continued to film in St Andrews after all the other press teams had left to allow William privacy. To make matters worse, the company was owned by the Prince's uncle, Prince Edward, and the incident left Charles furious. Ardent Productions soon apologised for the intrusion, and William continued his studies uninterrupted.

During his first year of study, William stayed in St Salvator's Hall, one of the university's halls of residences, which provided catered food and en-suite facilities. He had enrolled under the name 'William Wales', and other students nicknamed him 'Steve' to try and protect him from prying journalists. The principal of St Andrews, Dr Brian Lang, had previously warned students to avoid talking to the media about William, under the risk of being kicked out.

William struggled to adjust at St Andrews for the first term, and admitted that he initially had doubts about staying. However, after talking to his father, William decided to stick it out, acknowledging that most first-

TOP The building where William was to study for his history of art degree, although he eventually decided to change his subject to geography

MIDDLE William loved to play sports, and was a keen water polo player in particular

RIGHT Prince William is pictured here with his father, after receiving his degree at the graduation ceremony

ABOVE Queen Elizabeth II thankfully managed to attend Prince William's graduation ceremony in June 2005, after worries that illness might prevent her from doing so

> "He remained positive that he would be able to live the life of an ordinary student"

year students struggle with university life to begin with. He also chose to make the decision to switch from history of art to geography, which helped him to settle down.

William made a few close friends during his first year at university, and in the second year he decided to move out of halls and into a flat in Hope Street, which he shared with three other people: Fergus Boyd, Olivia Bleasdale and Kate Middleton. The Prince enjoyed his new domestic lifestyle, and revealed in an interview that he regularly cooked meals for the rest of his housemates.

William enjoyed playing sports during his free time, and was a member of the water polo team. He was picked to represent the university in April 2004 at the Celtic Nations tournament in Cardiff against Wales and Ireland in water polo after taking part in a set of trials, having missed previous opportunities because of other commitments. At the time, William was offered his own changing rooms for privacy but, in keeping with his desire to be an ordinary student, the prince declined this offer. Unfortunately, William's team lost to Ireland with a score of 14 – 7.

For the last two years of his degree, William moved into a four-bedroom house at the edge of town with his three housemates. William hoped to earn a 2:1 in his degree, but said that it all depended on his 10,000-word dissertation on the coral reefs of Rodrigues. Like every other university student across the country, William waited anxiously for his results. On 11 June 2005, it was announced that the Prince had earned the 2:1 he wanted, after logging on to the internet at Clarence House. As the announcement was made, he was attending the Trooping of the Colour with the rest of the royal family.

As the news of William's success spread, many commentators noted that the Prince had earned a better result than his father, who received a 2:2 in his history degree. William graduated on 23 June 2005, alongside 259 other students. He picked up his degree, a geography MA, in front of nearly 800 guests, as well as his grandparents, Queen Elizabeth II and Prince Philip, and his father and step-mother, Camilla. It was believed to be the first time that the Queen had ever attended a graduation for a family member, and there were fears that she might miss the occasion because of an illness she was suffering from near the time. Luckily, she pulled through in time to see her eldest grandson graduate in a black silk gown with a cherry, silk lining, indicating that he was now a Master of Arts.

After the ceremony, the royal family stayed to meet some of William's fellow students and their relatives. It was also announced that the Prince would be undertaking his first-ever solo public engagement, flying to New Zealand to commemorate the 60th anniversary of the end of World War II on behalf of the Queen.

William's time at university signalled the last time that he would live in relative seclusion, as his public role became more and more prominent at the end of his studies. The Prince now admits that there were times at university where he was a bit lazy, but continues to speak of his time at university with very fond memories, particularly as it is where he met, and fell in love with Kate.

An OFFICER and a GENTLEMAN

A career in the military was inevitable for William. He was set to follow in the footsteps of his father, grandfather and great-grandfather, and future head of the armed services will be his ultimate duty

A royal prince invariably ends up in the services. The link between military prowess and royalty is old and well established Even in modern times, senior royals are expected to undertake some form of service with the armed forces, and William was no exception. His father, the King had extensive military experience, while his paternal grandfather Prince Philip had seen active service in World War II. The founder of the House of Windsor, George V, had been a passionate navy man. The path to active service was mapped out for the young prince from the beginning.

The fun of dressing up in fatigues while playing at home in Highgrove, and the chance to try out tanks for real on visits like that made to Combermere in Windsor in the late Eighties were tasters of what was to come. William did well as a member of the Eton Rifles, winning the prestigious Sword of Honour as best cadet.

In his gap year between Eton and St Andrews University, William participated in army training exercises in Belize. He hoped to move on, eventually, to the Royal Military Academy Sandhurst to train as an officer, and was sure he had made the academic grade with his three A levels and potential university degree.

The military academy traces its origins back over 200 years and that history has seen it welcome many royal cadets. The prince's maternal grandfather also attended. However, family links were no help to William in winning admission to the academy, whose motto is 'Serve to Lead'. He had to pass the Regular Commissions Board before he could enter.

This four-day session is held near Westbury, Wiltshire, and it provided an instant reminder for William that in the armed services a royal title was no advantage. At the start of the tests, he was told he'd be known by a number, not his name, and judged against a standard. The second in line to the throne joined Sandhurst on 8 January 2006 and his passing out parade took place on 15 December 2006 in front of his grandmother Queen Elizabeth II, with the prince wearing the red sash as his platoon had earned the honour of carrying the Sovereign's banner.

William was immediately commissioned into cavalry unit the Blues and Royals as a cornet (second lieutenant) at the end of his time at Sandhurst. He had briefly considered joining the Irish Guards before following his brother into the cavalry. Both had been drawn to the Blues and Royals (Royal Horse Guards and 1st Dragoons) because of its role in

RIGHT Prince William, then Flight Lieutenant William Wales, pictured in June 2009 when he was learning to pilot a Griffin helicopter at the then Defence Helicopter Flying School at RAF Shawbury (Now No. 1 Flying Training School)

Image: Getty

TOP LEFT
Just before his wedding in April 2011, Prince William welcomed his grandmother to RAF Valley, where he was stationed as a search and rescue pilot

TOP RIGHT
Prince William during a training exercise on a Sea King helicopter – he would pilot the craft many times in difficult conditions

front-line reconnaissance work. With the conflicts in Iraq and Afghanistan still raging, the prince was focused on fighting for the country, even if it was already clear that the heir would stand little chance of fulfilling this ambition.

Straight out of Sandhurst, William started work as a troop commander in an armoured reconnaissance unit. This involved intensive training at the Royal Armoured Corps Centre at Bovington Camp in Dorset. As the prince born to be king, he was aware that his future role would see him become head of the armed services. He had only signed up for a short-term commission lasting three years. It was decided that some of that should provide William with experience of all three services and train him for the role he would one day take on.

The prince had never made any secret of his love of flying. Even before going to Sandhurst, he had spent time with the RAF Valley Mountain Rescue Team, and had talked of his ambitions to be a pilot. In January 2008 he was stationed with 1 Squadron of 1 Elementary Flying Training School at RAF Cranwell in Lincolnshire. Now known as Flying Officer William Wales, he embarked on four months of training with the RAF that quickly saw him take to the skies piloting solo flights.

The first plane he flew by himself was a Grob 115E light aircraft, but his short training course would see him take the controls of just about every plane in the service, including a Typhoon jet fighter. He won his RAF pilot wings in April 2007, with then then Kate Middleton in the audience for the presentation. Handing over the honour was William's father, then the Prince of Wales, who had also gone through similar training. William's next military step would yet again see him follow more family tradition.

In June 2008, he began a three-week course at the Britannia Royal Naval College in Dartmouth. Charles had also attended the prestigious training centre, as had William's great-grandfather, George VI, and great-great-grandfather, George V. Perhaps its most famous royal association in recent years had been as the place where the then Princess Elizabeth had first met her future husband Prince Philip on a visit in 1939.

The following weeks saw William train with surface fleet and submarine units, as well as with the Fleet Air Arm and the Royal Marines. From there he went to the West Indies for an operational attachment on HMS Iron Duke. The ship was positioned in the Caribbean in hurricane season for humanitarian purposes but also carried out work with the US Coast Guard in the hunt for drug smugglers.

During his time with the Iron Duke, William took part in a successful raid that ended with the capture of a gang in possession of around £40-million worth of cocaine. The five-week stint was an eye opener in many ways for William who, on his return to the UK, faced big decisions about his future.

The prospect of active service was fast fading for the then second in line to the throne, but his time with the RAF had seen William go to Afghanistan. The trip was brief, secret and poignant. He had been part of a crew that undertook a 30-hour mission to bring back the body of Robert Pearson, who had been killed in action. The sad journey ended at RAF Lyneham, where William asked to meet the parents of Trooper Pearson to offer them comfort.

In 2009, William and Harry were both training at the Defence Helicopter Flying School, where William was able to guide Harry as he got to grips with some of the training he'd already undertaken.

William graduated in January 2010, with Harry following him in May of the same year.

From RAF Shawbury, William moved to RAF Valley on Anglesey, where he began training on Sea King search and rescue helicopters. In April 2010, he was assigned to C Flight No. 22 Squadron for an operational tour set to last up to three years. Initially a co-pilot, William soon began taking part in missions. Early rescue efforts saw him involved in an operation at an offshore gas rig near Morecambe Bay, and helping rescue sailors from a sinking cargo ship in the Irish Sea. The posting on the Welsh island also helped William and Kate embrace the home nation of which they would one day be Prince and Princess.

By now, the chances of William seeing frontline military service were beginning to fade fast, although a six-week tour of the Falkland Islands in 2012 with No. 1564 Flight proved controversial after Argentina described it as a provocative act, coming so close to the 30th anniversary of the conflict in the islands that began with Argentina's invasion attempt.

BELOW William and Harry both trained at the Defence Helicopter Flying School at RAF Shawbury in 2009, and shared a cottage nearby while completing their studies

> "Family links were no help in winning admission to the Sandhurst academy"

Harry and William had, from an early age, taken a deep interest in the plight of wounded service personnel. The princes had already given their support to the campaign Help for Heroes, which had begun to raise funds to help those being treated at Headley Court, the military rehabilitation unit in Surrey. In 2007, William and Harry asked for it to be a beneficiary of the premiere of the James Bond film *Quantum of Solace*, which they were due to attend, and the following year they helped inspire a fundraiser for the charity and the Soldiers, Sailors, Airmen and Families Association in London, which brought in £1 million.

Both had made trips to Headley Court to meet wounded service personnel, while William had spoken movingly as early as 2004 about the importance of remembering those who had made the ultimate sacrifice for their country. Prince Harry announced the creation of the Invictus Games in March 2014, which would celebrate the sporting achievements of those who had suffered physical and emotional injuries while serving with their country's armed forces. Supported by money from the Royal Foundation of the Duke and Duchess of Cambridge (William and Kate's titles at the time) and Prince Harry, the project quickly built up a head of steam, and in September 2014, four days of events saw around 300 competitors from 14 countries compete..

The Invictus Games proved to be far more of a success than Prince Harry had ever imagined, and in July 2015, it was confirmed that a second set of Invictus Games would take place in Orlando in 2016.

By this time however, Prince William's military career was over. His active service as a search and rescue pilot ended in 2013, but William then chose to take a two-year contract as an air ambulance pilot.

Although a civilian job, it called on many of the skills he had learned in his military career, and his two years with the East Anglian Air Ambulance would see him involved in many rescue missions, often piloting helicopters in treacherous conditions. An heir to the throne working to save lives in the emergency services captured the public imagination at home and abroad.

His experiences in the armed forces have clearly shaped how William sees his future royal roles. The focus on providing support for those experiencing mental-health problems following service – highlighted as part of William and Harry's Heads Together campaign – underlines the importance the prince places on the value of the Army, Royal Navy and the RAF.

WILLIAM'S CHARITABLE *contributions*

Using the world's scrutiny and fascination in the royal family's every move as a means to promote causes that really matter is a tactic first perfected by William's mother, and her legacy is continued today thanks to the efforts of the Prince of Wales

Royal patronage – the official association and support between a member of the royal family and an organisation – dates back to George II's reign, when he became involved with the Society of Antiquaries. It is a tradition that has increased significantly over the years, and now some 3,000 organisations, ranging from well-known international bodies to small local groups, have a member of the royal family as their patron or president.

Prince William and Prince Harry have both proved enthusiastic in their charity work, becoming patron or president of hundreds of charities. By associating their names and lending their backing to shine the media spotlight on their targeted causes, they give a significant boost in publicity and awareness. However, they have also diversified their means of pursuing philanthropic causes by hosting and attending one-off events, such as concerts – for instance the Concert for Diana – and the Invictus Games. These large-scale events rally support from celebrities and the public, and raise significant amounts of money for a range of charitable pursuits.

In addition, as they have gathered a significant collection of charities under their patronage, they have established an umbrella organisation with which to promote collaboration and cooperation between the charities they head. Started in 2006, the Charities Forum now involves 30 organisations that can use the Forum as a way of interacting, sharing ideas and pooling resources for mutually applicable events and projects. It is an intelligent initiative that is designed to help organisations pull together to achieve their individual and shared goals.

In 2015, for example, Centrepoint, which Prince William is patron of, and his former patronage the Child Bereavement Charity, joined forces with WellChild, whose patron was Prince Harry, to host outdoor activities for children and families who had been helped by all the charities involved – a joint initiative to provide enjoyment and relief for vulnerable people that was made possible through the improved cooperation brought about by the Charities Forum.

In a similar vein, the princes also established the Royal Foundation, although Harry has now left the organisation. Started in 2009, it aims to become the "primary charitable vehicle and hopes to become a leading philanthropic investor, effectively using its time and resources to create lasting change in targeted areas and geographies". Essentially, it is a means of managing a multitude

RIGHT The then 19-year-old Prince William on a Raleigh International expedition on his gap year between Eton and St Andrews University. He visited Chile, where he is seen here working on a local radio station building in Tortel

Image: Getty

of philanthropic endeavours by centralising funding and systems of support that can be distributed to the individual charities.

It is also used as a vehicle with which to garner support from significant parties and lobby government support. One example is the Cyberbullying Taskforce, which aims to raise awareness and actively pull together tech giants to combat the growing problem of bullying online, especially among young people. The Royal Foundation united groups, charities and companies, including The Anti-Bullying Alliance, Apple, BT, The Diana Award, EE, Facebook, Google, Internet Matters, NSPCC, O2, Sky, Snapchat, Supercell, TalkTalk, Twitter, Vodafone and Virgin Media. These hugely influential players have been brought together to take action, all supported and united under the auspices of the Royal Foundation.

William throws his support behind charities and events that broadly follow three main causes, which are specified both in the Charities Forum's and the Royal Foundation's websites: 'supporting members of the armed forces and their families, helping children and young people, and promoting conservation and sustainable development'.

The prioritisation of charities helping children and young people is a powerful example of the lasting influence and legacy of William's mother. Princess Diana was perhaps the first 'celebrity' royal, endlessly tailed by paparazzi, with huge swathes of newspaper columns dedicated to reporting her every action to an enthralled audience. Diana learnt how to utilise this attention to promote causes that meant something to her – none more so than the welfare of children around the world. This has directly influenced the Prince of Wales' charitable pursuits.

As already mentioned, William is the patron of Centrepoint, a charity helping young people who are homeless or at risk of living on the streets. It provides accommodation, health and education support to some of the country's most vulnerable young people. In this he has followed directly in the footsteps of his mother, who became patron of Centrepoint in 1992, one of only six charities she did not resign from after her divorce from the hundred she previously patronised while still married.

Prince William was taken to Centrepoint bases and events by his mother, and has talked about its lasting impact on him: "That really struck me at a young age, bearing in mind the gulf for me, growing up in a palace, and seeing the other end of the spectrum where others were faced with huge personal challenges and were overcoming them. That was powerful to see at a young age."

Continuing his mother's work with the charity, William regularly attends events with Centrepoint, speaking with the young people, volunteers and workers involved in the charity. In 2009, the prince slept rough for a night alongside Centrepoint's CEO, Seyi Obakin, in an attempt to begin to appreciate the conditions many young people find themselves in. Temperatures reportedly reached as low as minus four on London's wintry streets – a very far cry from the glamorous halls and plush rooms of the regal Kensington Palace, residing in the same city but a world away from life on the streets. William also became patron of The Passage, the UK's largest resource centre for homeless and insecurely housed people, in February 2019, showing further commitment to tackling the problem of homelessness in Great Britain.

When Prince William assumed the role of president at The Royal Marsden

RIGHT Prince William goes on a fell walk in Cumbria alongside homeless people who are being assisted by Centrepoint, 2009

Hospital in 2007, he again filled a role held by his mother, who had assumed the role of president in 1989 until her death. The Royal Marsden Hospital provides specialist care for children with cancer, and was the first hospital in the world dedicated to specialist cancer research and treatment. Enjoying a long association with the royal family, it was granted the royal title by George V. Prince William's association with the hospital has allowed him to lend support through his money-raising events and organisations. Prince William had been involved in the hospital before becoming president, even undertaking two days of work experience in 2005 in the children's unit at the age of 23.

Both William and Harry have also actively supported the Concert for Diana and the Diana Awards. The Concert for Diana in 2007 was broadcast in 140 countries and raised money for the charities chosen by the two princes, including Centrepoint.

It is not only their mother who has helped to shape their beliefs and causes. Their focus on conservation closely follows the actions of their father, King Charles III. Charles has long supported conservation and sustainability projects, such as being patron to the WWF and the Zoological Society of London.

His sons also have this cause embedded in them, and the theme runs through their patronages and charitable pursuits. For example, Prince William has been the patron of the Tusk Trust since 2005. It is a charity that funds conservation, encourages environmental education across Africa, and promotes sustainability. Among his actions, William has given keynote speeches at high-profile events, such as the premiere of *African Cats*, in order to raise the profile of the Tusk Trust. It also, incidentally, helps to continue Prince William's connection to Africa. William was quoted as saying "the continent completely settles me down" after proposing to Kate in Kenya. He has also assumed the presidency of United for Wildlife, a Royal Foundation initiative that has brought some of the largest conservation organisations together to collaborate on projects, in particular engaging a younger audience for environmental education and awareness, and harnessing new technologies to reach a new audience.

The final cause both William and Harry have prioritised, the support of servicemen and their families, is mainly derived from their own experiences in the military. Both have actively served in the armed forces: William was a Guards officer and helicopter pilot for seven years until 2013. Both have subsequently given up their positions.

Despite giving up their military positions, they have maintained a close bond with the armed forces. Prince Harry was a patron of Walking With The Wounded, a charity that helps servicemen and ex-servicemen readjust into society after suffering injury or mental illness, or facing difficulties since leaving the military, and attended several high-profile expeditions with military veterans in order to raise awareness, such as an expedition to the North Pole in 2011, the South Pole in 2013 and a Walk Across Britain event in 2015.

The Prince of Wales has a sprawling web of charitable pursuits through which he uses his position of influence to further worthy causes. The Princess of Wales has also added her philanthropic pursuits to the Royal Foundation framework established by the princes. Together they will continue to change countless lives such as with Heads Together, which was launched in 2016 to tackle the issue of mental health.

BELOW Prince William and Harry come to grips with an African rock python on a charity tour. Their tour took them to Botswana, Lesotho and South Africa, conducting visits to their various charities across the region

> *"William was taken to Centrepoint bases by his mother, and has talked about its impact"*

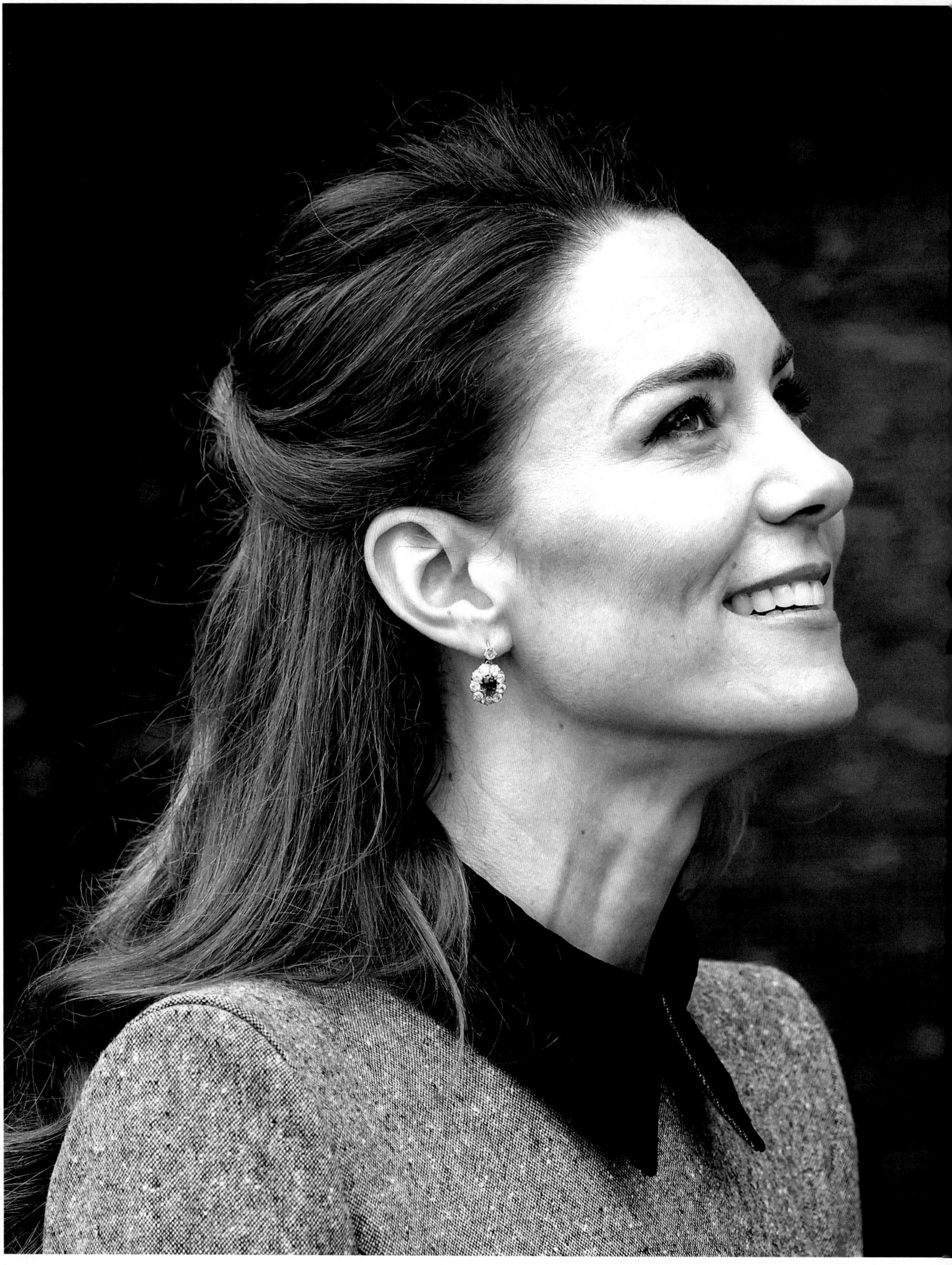

056 .... The Making of a Duchess
062 .... Student Days
070 .... Kate Goes to Work
074 .... Caring Kate's Causes and Charities

CATHERINE
Princess of Wales

The MAKING of a DUCHESS

Born to hard-working parents who ensured that she enjoyed every benefit that money could buy, the reserved and quiet Kate Middleton was destined for a golden future. However, the poised and beautiful duchess that we all know and admire today was once forced to change schools after being bullied – an experience left her feeling shy and anxious

When flight despatcher Michael Middleton and his wife Carole, whom he had met when they were both working as British Airways flight attendants, welcomed their first child in the Royal Berkshire Hospital maternity unit in Reading on the 9 January 1982, they never could have predicted that their new baby daughter would one day become one of the most famous women in the world.

After being discharged from hospital, the Middleton family returned to their modest Victorian semi-detached house on Cock Lane in the village of Bradfield Southend in Berkshire, which they had bought a few months before their wedding on 21 June 1980. Their baby girl was christened Catherine Elizabeth in the local church, St Andrew's, on 20 June 1982 when she was six months old. Just over a year later, Kate was joined on 6 September 1983 by a sister, Philippa, better known as Pippa.

While Kate's mother, Carole, came from an ordinary working-class family and attended state school in Southall, West London, her father, Michael, came from a wealthy middle-class background and went to the prestigious Clifton College public school in Bristol, which had also been attended by his father and grandfather. While Carole has miners, farm labourers, butchers, road sweepers and even convicts in her family tree (along with Guy Ritchie and Helena Bonham-Carter, who are both very distant cousins), Michael is related to Victorian writer Harriet Martineau and has wealthy mill owners, politicians, mayors and even minor nobility in his ancestry. However, although their backgrounds on paper were rather different, Carole and Michael were clearly a match made in heaven and shared the same values, ambition and willingness to work hard to achieve their goals.

While Carole gave up work to look after her daughters, Michael continued to work for British Airways and in 1984, when Kate was just two years old, accepted a promotion that involved the family relocating to Amman, the capital of Jordan, where Kate attended an English-language nursery school and learned how to sing Happy Birthday in Arabic, to the delight of her parents and relatives at home. They lived there until September 1986 before returning to their home in Bradfield Southend, when Carole was expecting their third child – their only son James was born seven months later on 15 April 1987, completing their close knit family group.

Carole did not return to British Airways, but instead, decided to start her own business, founding Party Pieces in 1987. The mail order company

RIGHT Kate loved to be outside and active from a very young age as demonstrated by this family photograph of her exploring a rock face during a holiday in the Lake District when she was three and a half years old

Image: Getty

originally supplied party favour bags, inspired by the ones that she had been creating for her daughters' birthday parties, but eventually branched out into more general party supplies and decorations. Like most businesses, it took a while for Party Pieces to become established but it steadily became more popular and by the early nineties, Michael had given up his job at British Airways in order to work alongside Carole.

While their parents concentrated on the family business, the three Middleton children attended the Bradfield Church of England primary school just a few doors down from their house. The house was rapidly becoming too small for the family and the demands of Carole's business, which she initially dealt with single-handedly, putting together orders and sending them out from her garden shed.

Kate was a popular resident of the village, where she sang in the church choir and, along with her sister Pippa, was a member of the 1st St Andrew's Brownie pack, which involved participating in camping trips. By 1990, when Kate was eight, Party Pieces was successful enough for the Middleton children to be sent to the private St Andrew's school in nearby Pangbourne, where Kate was initially a day pupil before boarding for her last two years.

St Andrew's wasn't an especially academic school – its emphasis was more on making its pupils as polite, punctual and well spoken as possible, with marked success when it came to Kate and her sister Pippa, who were both renowned for always turning up on time and then staying late to help tidy up after games lessons and school events. Kate particularly loved her time at St Andrew's, where she was given the nickname Squeak (her younger sister Pippa, with whom she was very close, was obviously 'Pip'), and told her mother that one day she would return there as a teacher as she had loved it so much.

LEFT When Kate was two years old, the family temporarily relocated to Amman, the capital of Jordan, where Kate attended an English-language nursery school.

> "Kate was a popular resident of the village, where she sang in the church choir"

At St Andrew's, Kate was one of the stars of the school choir, learned to play the flute and piano (although she didn't progress past Grade Three, despite taking extra lessons outside the school) and always participated in the annual skiing trips, where she learned to become an expert skier. Although her chief love was for sport, Kate also found the time to apply a great deal of diligence to her studies, often staying late to do her homework. However, her nemesis was Craft Design Technology, which she absolutely hated as she could never quite get to grips with the practical side of the lessons.

Her time at her next school, the exclusive all girls Downe House, where she started as a day pupil in September 1995, was much less happy, however. Kate had discovered a passion for sport, particularly hockey, at St Andrew's school and was dismayed to discover that it was not played there and that she would instead be expected to play lacrosse, a game that she was not familiar with. She was also tormented by other girls at the school, who had decided that she didn't fit in, probably because she was a day pupil while most of the others were boarders. She also suffered with eczema and was unusually tall for her age, which made her stand out. Her time at Downe House was miserable thanks to the other girls pointedly excluding her and pushing her around, which destroyed her confidence.

In the end, after just two terms, the desperately unhappy Kate was removed by her parents and instead sent to the co-educational and far more prestigious boarding school Marlborough College in Wiltshire,

RIGHT The young Kate Middleton (front left) was captain of the hockey team at St Andrew's preparatory school and her love for the sport has remained constant ever since.

where she quickly began to flourish thanks to the kindness of her teachers and peers, and was encouraged to pursue her interest in sport, especially her beloved hockey as well as tennis (at which she excelled), swimming, cross country and netball.

At St Andrew's, she had been the highest scorer in the rounders team, captain of the hockey team, competed at swimming and set a high jump record that remains unbeaten even now – all of which earned her a trophy for outstanding sporting achievement. At Marlborough she continued to impress everyone with her sporting prowess and enthusiasm. She also completed her Duke of Edinburgh award, especially relishing the more gruelling outdoor challenges such as a four day hike in the rain and gaining her gold award – which was presented to her by the Duke of Edinburgh himself in St James' Palace.

To everyone's relief, Kate clearly found Marlborough College much more congenial and, after feeling initially very shy because of her unhappy experience at Downe House, settled in and made plenty of friends, who would later remember her as a good natured, intelligent, sporty and very likeable girl who loved microwaved Marmite sandwiches, blueberry muffins and Pepperami, did an excellent impression of Cilla Black, idolised Kate Moss and had a huge crush on the actor Tom Cruise, but took very little interest in the boys that she saw every day at school – her chief passion in life was still sport.

While Kate and her siblings were moving through the school system, their parents were also on the move when, thanks to the success of Party Pieces, they were able to sell the house in Bradfield Southend, and buy the much more imposing Oak Acre, a detached five-bedroom Tudor-style country house in the village of Bucklebury, ten miles away. The new house came with one and a half acres of land and was surrounded by countryside, which meant that the young Middletons could indulge their love for running and long walks – which they also enjoyed during regular family holidays to the Lake District, Barbados or to various ski resorts overseas. While at home during the holidays and weekends, Kate helped out with the family business, which had grown too big for her parents' house and was now based in old farm buildings nearby.

Kate had always loved inviting friends back to their house in Bradfield Southend, where she enjoyed baking cakes and biscuits for her guests, and the new house offered much more space to entertain. She did this with gusto, inviting school friends back for parties in the huge garage, which her parents had converted into a games room and where they could make as much noise as they liked, with Kate being especially fond of loud rap music and impromptu singalongs.

At Marlborough, although she excelled in all sports, with one school friend later commenting that 'there was hardly a sport that she didn't play', Kate also loved to participate in the school's regular programme of

"Like a lot of girls at the time, she was fascinated by Prince William, who was the same age as her"

dramatic productions, having gained a taste for drama while playing Eliza Doolittle in a production of *My Fair Lady* at St Andrew's school. Like many other shy people, she clearly appreciated the fact that acting gave her an opportunity to step outside herself for a while and pretend to be someone else, as well as helping her to feign confidence in front of an audience – which she would find very useful in her later life as a royal duchess. She would also love painting and it was almost certainly at this time that she discovered her passion for photography.

Academically, Kate was also a high achiever, working hard to gain 11 GCSEs in 1998 and then 3 A Levels in Chemistry, Biology and Art in 2000. Although her schoolmates would later talk about the fun that they got up to after school hours in the Marlborough dormitories, it's clear that Kate was never very into partying while at school but instead preferred to concentrate on sport and studying, with one friend later remarking that she very rarely saw her drunk. Like her parents, she was extremely ambitious and determined to make the most of the opportunities that her education had given her. Like a lot of girls at the time, she was fascinated by Prince William, who was the same age as her, but although she expressed a desire to meet him and even joined in banter with her friends about what it would be like to marry him one day, it's unlikely that she had any expectations about one day becoming his wife.

After she finished her A Levels, Kate decided to defer making a decision about where to attend university and instead opted to enjoy a gap year while she considered her future plans. In September 2000, when many of her peers were setting off to start their degrees, she travelled to Florence in Italy and enrolled on a 12-week

LEFT
A photograph of five-year-old Kate, just after she had started school

LEFT Idyllic Bucklebury in West Berkshire, where the Middleton family lived from Kate's early teens. It was one of the backdrops to the early years of her relationship with Prince William

course at the British Institute on the Piazza Strozzi, where she studied Italian and History of Art in the magnificent surroundings of the Renaissance Palazzo dello Strozzino and Palazzo Lanfredini. Kate loved Florence, where she shared a small flat above a delicatessen with three other students and spent three hours every day studying the Italian language, as well as enjoying guided tours around the wonderful Florentine palaces, museums and churches and trips to nearby Siena and Pisa. Kate loved to spend hours roaming around Florence, taking photos and visiting galleries – she was already strongly leaning towards studying History of Art at university, and this trip to Florence convinced her that it would be the perfect course.

In the evenings, Kate would often be seen at the popular L'Art Bar in the city centre where she would enjoy cocktails with her friends, although as at Marlborough, she was never seen to get very drunk and was adept at avoiding the attentions of amorous locals, preferring instead to spend time with an old school boyfriend called Harry. Six weeks into her course, her parents came out to visit her in Florence and she proudly showed them around the city before taking her friends to meet them for drinks in their hotel. After leaving Florence, Kate then joined a Rayleigh International expedition to Patagonia in Chile for ten weeks, where she helped to build a fire station and taught English to children at a local school. When she returned home to the UK, Kate worked as crew on a boat taking part in the BT Global Challenge in the Solent, which was physically tough work but also a lot of fun.

When this ended, she joined her family for a fortnight in Holetown, Barbados, which was one of their favourite holiday destinations – it was the perfect end to what had been an extremely busy gap year and gave her time to relax before she embarked on the next important phase of her life.

Images: Getty

STUDENT DAYS

After a gap year spent exploring Chile and Florence, Kate headed to university to spend four years studying history of art. Although she had heard Prince William would also be there, not even in her wildest dreams could she have predicted that they would end up falling in love

Like most of her school friends, Kate spent the last year of her A-levels trying to decide what she wanted to study at university and, perhaps more crucially, where she wanted to go. As she took two science A-levels, it seemed likely that she would carry on with science at university, so it may have come as a surprise when she announced that she was thinking about doing history of art instead. Although Edinburgh, which has an excellent history of art department, was her first choice, she was also considering St Andrews, another Scottish university, along with Oxford Brookes and a few others. When she left for her gap year she had still not decided where to study. However, by the time she returned from her adventures in Florence and South America, her mind was made up and she accepted an offer from the University of St Andrews to study history of art. It would be suggested afterwards that Kate's decision to switch from Edinburgh to St Andrews was prompted by the announcement that Prince William was planning to enrol there too, in order to study history of art, but it was almost certainly just coincidence that brought them there at the same time – although Kate was undoubtedly ambitious, deciding to switch universities on the off chance that she might meet William really wasn't her style at all.

Kate enrolled at St Andrews in autumn 2001 and was given a room in the picturesque gothic St Salvator's Hall in the centre of town. Although there was an option to have her own room, she opted to share and ended up with Sarah Bates, who became a close friend, as a roommate. The two girls shared a room on the first floor, which had a communal kitchen along with separate shared showers. The dining room, reading room and oak-panelled common room, which had a grand piano and television, were all downstairs along with laundry facilities. When the new undergraduates first arrived they had no idea that Prince William would be living with them until a few days into Fresher's Week, when they were gathered together in the common room and told that he would be arriving the following week. He had decided not to partake in Fresher's Week in case his presence ruined everyone else's fun. Although Kate, like most of the other students in St Salvator's Hall, must have been excited

RIGHT Kate looked as poised and elegant as ever when she arrived for her graduation ceremony at St Andrews on 23 June 2005

> *"Switching universities on the off chance that she might meet William really wasn't her style at all"*

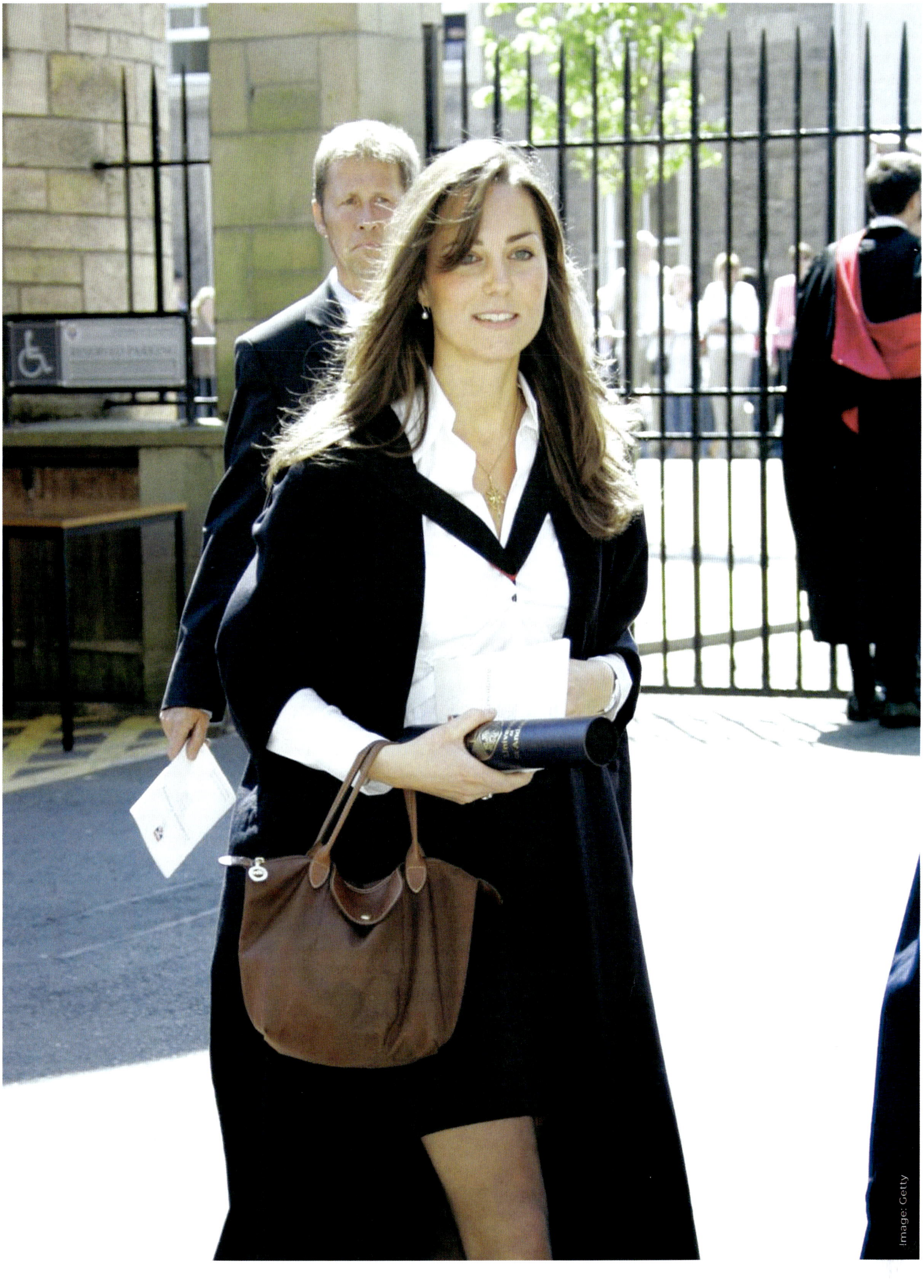

Image: Getty

"*It was Kate who photocopied her lecture notes and helped him catch up with his coursework*"

that William would be living nearby, she had already been distracted by the handsome Rupert Finch, who was just starting the final year of his law degree. Meanwhile, William lost very little time before acquiring a new girlfriend. He could hardly have failed to notice the willowy and very beautiful Kate Middleton though, who not only lived downstairs from him but was doing the same course. Obviously it helped that she had been unofficially crowned the prettiest girl in their halls at the start of the year. For now, though, the two were just friends, although they spent increasing amounts of time together as the year progressed, with Kate becoming one of the very few women allowed into William's close inner circle of friends, most of whom he had known at Eton. At first the pair would just chat occasionally after lectures but gradually these brief exchanges turned into regular evening catch ups in the common room, excursions to the pub and having muesli together in the mornings before they headed to lectures. Like Kate, William was excellent at sport and loved to be outdoors in all weathers and they would regularly watch the university rugby and hockey teams together, go swimming in a local health club or enjoy a long walk by the sea talking about their shared experiences. William had also gone out to Peru for his gap year, but had left just before Kate's arrival. When William had to return home for official events, it was Kate who photocopied her lecture notes and helped him catch up with his coursework and gradually he began to rely on her. When William admitted in the middle of his first year that he wasn't enjoying university life and disliked his course, Kate persuaded him to switch to geography – always his strongest subject anyway – and stay on at St Andrews.

For her part, Kate did not share William's dissatisfaction with their course and loved studying history of art, regarding it as a privilege to be able to spend her time immersed in beautiful art and learning more about the great masters. Unlike William, who felt unable to really let his hair down and have fun with the other students, Kate threw herself into university life, even getting so drunk at a ball that she had to be carried home. She was still shy and extremely reserved but had no difficulty making friends and quickly became a popular part of the student body, throwing herself into various extra-curricular activities, especially her beloved sport, but was also punctilious about attending every lecture and seminar.

At the end of their first year, Kate signed up to take part in the annual student fashion show, not realising that she would be expected to wear a completely see-through black dress, that was originally intended to be worn as a skirt. Prince William had refused to take part in the event but had an excellent view of Kate from his front-row seat, which he had paid £200 for. Although he can't have failed to note just how beautiful his friend was, the sight of her in a transparent dress seemed to have a huge impact on him and he exclaimed to one of his friends about how 'hot' she looked. However, when the intoxicated William leaned in to kiss Kate at the after party, she gently rebuffed him, not least because she was still seeing Finch – for the time being at least, as the couple split up

LEFT Kate graduated St Andrews with a 2:1 history of art degree, which would serve her well in her brief career after leaving university

RIGHT It was big smiles all round on that graduation day in 2005, with William receiving his geography degree along with Kate

Images: Getty

after Finch graduated and moved to London a few months later.

When Kate and William got together shortly afterwards, none of their close friends were even remotely surprised, although they managed to keep the romance quiet for a fair amount of time to come, aided by the fact that they shared a house on Hope Street with their friends Fergus Boyd and Olivia Bleasdale during their second year. If William seemed to spend more time with one of his housemates than the others, then hardly anyone outside their close-knit group of friends appeared to notice. Although the press had been banned from harassing William and his friends in St Andrews, a few rogue photographers still broke the rules by taking photos of the Prince during term time, but to everyone's relief and amusement they never cottoned on to the fact that Kate was his girlfriend. Instead, they reported that a different girl, who was on William's course and was photographed walking to the shops with him, had caught the Prince's eye.

By now William was happily studying geography so they saw less of each other during the day, but when lectures were over the pair were often to be found hanging out together in the popular student bars of Ma Bells or the Gin House, or attending one of the numerous student balls held during the summer months. Kate and William were at the centre of a social group that mostly comprised the wealthiest, public-school-educated students at St Andrews but whereas some of their peers were thought to be noisy, arrogant and snobbish by the other students, William and Kate were, perhaps surprisingly, regarded by most as being the most approachable members of their clique. When not in the bar, they mostly kept to themselves and preferred going for long walks on the beach, playing tennis, riding around on William's motorbike or enjoying quiet dinners together or getting drunk. When William decided

ABOVE Kate shared a room on the first floor of beautiful St Salvator's Hall in St Andrews, while William had his own en suite room two floors above her

"When the intoxicated William leaned in to kiss Kate at the after party, she gently rebuffed him"

to resume playing rugby, Kate was always there on the sidelines to cheer him on and he returned the favour when she played hockey with the university team. The couple also loved to host simple dinner parties in their shared flat, with Kate being by far the better cook while William, who preferred to drink and act as host, usually decided to play it safe and stick to pasta when it was his turn in the kitchen. When William became a member of an all-male drinking club, Kate retaliated by forming a female-only equivalent, which she decided to name the Lumsden Club after Dame Louisa Lumsden, a prominent Victorian educationalist.

At weekends, William was fond of whisking Kate up north to the cottage that he and his brother Harry had been given on the Balmoral estate. There, they could be completely alone and enjoy the glorious scenery and plenty of time outside, which they both enjoyed. If they wanted to go to London then they often stayed in the flat that Kate's parents had bought as a pied-à-terre in Mayfair, which was much more discreet than staying over at one of the royal residences, although Kate stayed at Highgrove for the first time that summer, where she met William's father. When Kate turned 21 in January 2003, William was present at her Great Gatsby-themed birthday party at her parents' house in Bucklebury, but did his best to stay in the background and avoid any public gestures that might reveal just how close they actually were. Kate was also a guest at William's Out of Africa-themed 21st birthday party later in the same year, and once again they took measures to ensure that their relationship remained under wraps, although Kate could hardly have enjoyed seeing the subsequent newspaper articles that named a different female guest, his old friend Jecca Craig, as being his girlfriend, even suggesting that she was the guest of honour thanks to all the attention he was paying her.

In reality, Kate had nothing to worry about. They had already decided that when they returned to St Andrews in the summer they would be living together as a couple, rather than sharing a flat with friends. They chose the idyllic four-bedroomed Balgove House just outside town as their new home and settled into a life of domestic bliss — only mildly hampered by the security team in the cottage next door, 24-hour surveillance and CCTV cameras in every room, except the bedroom and bathroom. To further cement the seriousness of their relationship, William invited Kate to accompany him to a family skiing holiday in Klosters in April 2004. The trip itself was a huge success until an errant press photographer managed to capture a photograph of the couple snuggling up on a ski lift, which then appeared in the *Sun* and effectively let the cat out of the bag about William and Kate's relationship.

Now that their romance was no longer a secret, Kate really began to feel the pressure of media interest as reporters descended on Bucklebury in the hopes of cornering her parents. She also had to cope with a series of tawdry kiss-and-tell articles about young women who had encountered William in nightclubs as well as rumours that he was planning to dump her for one of the many aristocratic beauties in his social circle. 'He's lucky to be going out with me,' Kate told her friends when they expressed concern about the pressure that she was under, but it must have been a stressful time for her. The couple returned to Balgove House for their fourth and final year at St Andrews, during which Kate worked hard on her dissertation; 'Angels from Heaven: Lewis Carroll's Photographic Interpretation of Childhood', which required a great deal of work alongside the lectures that she had to attend every week as their final exams approached. As was traditional at St Andrews, they were both sprayed with a celebratory fizzy drink when they emerged from taking their final exams before heading off to the bar with their friends. Despite the external pressures on them that year, both Kate and William did well and managed to get 2:1 degrees, which they proudly received when they graduated on 23 June 2005 in the presence of William's grandparents, the Queen and Prince Philip, who had travelled up especially for the ceremony but who wouldn't be introduced to Kate, although they undoubtedly knew who she was. Charles and his new second wife, Camilla, entertained Kate's parents at dinner the night before, though, and they all watched proudly as first Kate and then, much later for they were called up alphabetically, William made their way on to the stage to receive their diploma. In his speech, Vice Chancellor Dr Brian Lang made a reference to the fact that a higher than average amount of St Andrews students ended up married to each other and although William had already publicly announced that he had no intention of getting married until he was much older, many people there must have wondered what was going to happen next in the great royal romance that they had watched unfolding over the last four years.

ABOVE Kate was voted the prettiest girl in her hall of residence and had many male admirers during her time spent at St Andrews

Clearly delighted and relieved to have finished their courses and finally graduated after four years of hard work, the young couple looked forward to whatever the future would bring

Image: Getty

KATE goes to WORK

Like other graduates who completed university in the mid 2000s, Kate's immediate life following the completion of her degree in History of Art involved gathering experience in entry-level jobs for a career in the arts. The intense press intrusion took a toll on Kate's career, but the experience prepared her for a life in the public eye

Kate Middleton's life before she became the Duchess of Cambridge and then Princess of Wales was hardly what you'd call normal – that was to say it did not mirror the life of most young people from the UK. Educated at one of the nation's top universities, there was already a strong chance that Kate would be well prepared for a rewarding and well-paying job. As the daughter of wealthy and loving parents who owned a multi-million-pound family business, she also knew that she would never find herself in a precarious financial situation.

What was different, however, was that Kate needed to work at all. William's mother, Diana, had worked for a short time in various roles as a playgroup assistant, a hostess and a nanny, but styled as a Lady as the daughter of an Earl in the prestigious Spencer family, there was little chance of her ever needing – or perhaps even wanting – to take up full-time professional work. Philip had been in the Navy during World War II and was stationed in Malta until George VI's illness in 1951, but this was a tradition of the upper classes and not something borne out of necessity.

By the time she left university in 2005, Kate had known William for four years and their relationship was still by

RIGHT Despite the pressures of being a royal girlfriend with an uncertain future, Kate had fun after completing her university degree

no means set in stone, their apparent decision to split up in April 2007 a case in point. Kate could not rely on the fact that she would marry William and have a job for life as a royal. Headstrong, she realised that she needed a career of her own.

The obvious place to start, given the keen interest in fashion that she had explored at university, as well as her love of art, was in the clothes and fashion business. In 2006, she began working at Jigsaw as an assistant accessories buyer at their Dover Street store in Mayfair. The brand was founded in 1970 by John Robinson, who opened the first Jigsaw store in Brighton and then in Hampstead two years later. Twice in 1989 and in 1990 the company won awards from the British Fashion Council for contemporary design of the year and for having 'More Dash Than Cash', respectively. Marketed as a company which deliberately does not follow the trends of other fashion brands but as a purveyor of clothes and accessories to the 'independent-minded and fun' fashionista, at the time Kate joined Jigsaw it was expanding rapidly. In

> *"Kate could not rely on marrying William – she realised that she needed a career of her own"*

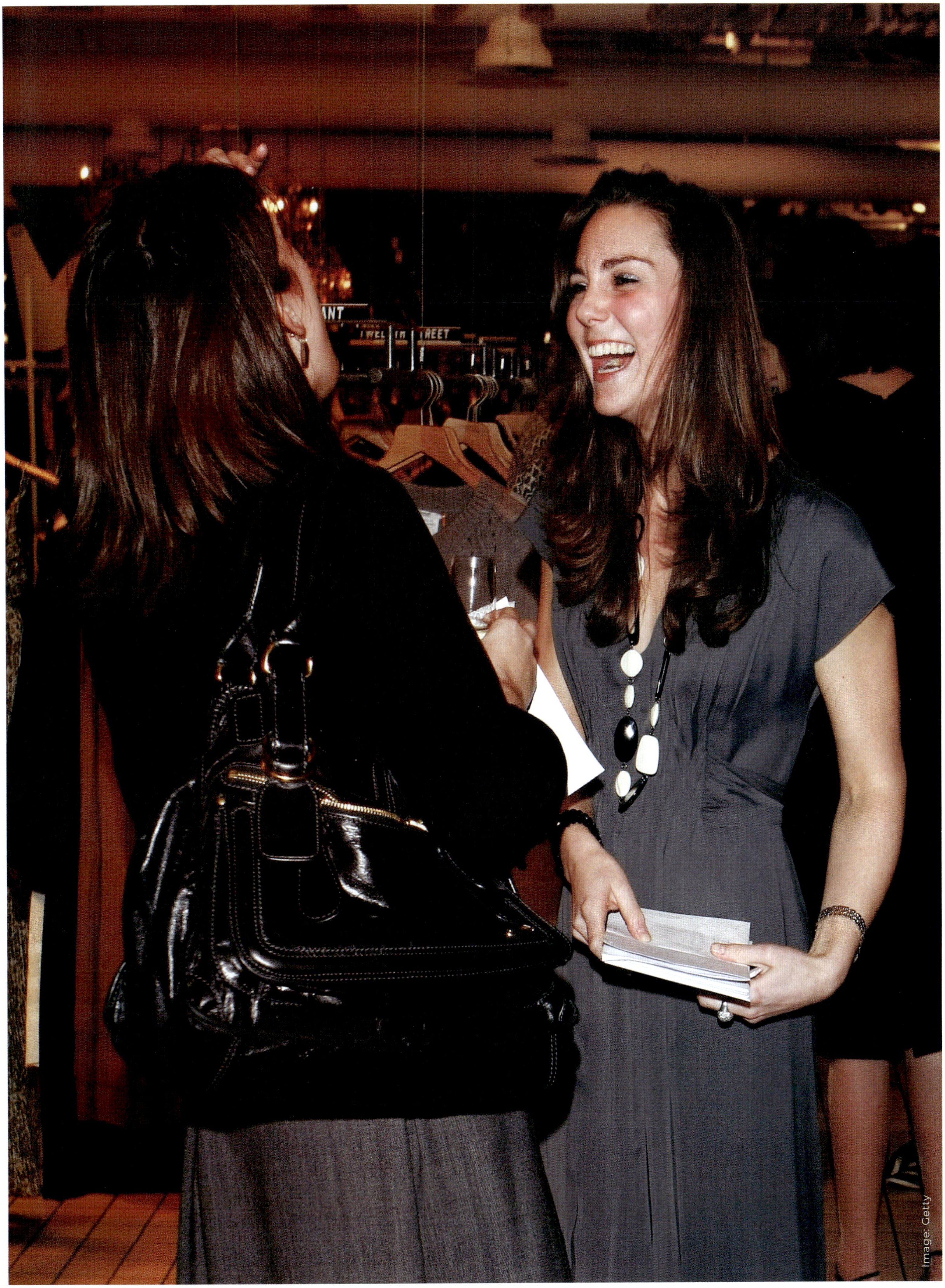

Image: Getty

2004, Jigsaw had opened their first US store in Los Angeles, and in 2005 they opened a 'concept store' on King's Road, London, known for its art deco high-end furniture and homeware brands, which were supposed to complement the clothes and accessories it buys.

John Robinson's wife, Belle, a partner in the business, was the woman who gave Kate her first break. As the Robinsons and Middletons were familiar, Kate and William asked if they could stay at their holiday home in Mustique. As a thank-you, Kate agreed to support some Jigsaw events. "[Kate] rang me up one day and said, 'Could I come and talk to you about work?'" says Belle. "She genuinely wanted a job but she needed an element of flexibility to continue the relationship with a very high-profile man and a life that she can't dictate. She's going to be dictated to when she's needed and not needed. And I have to say I was so impressed by her.

ABOVE The high-end Jigsaw fashion store. Kate worked briefly as a fashion accessories buyer for three days a week at their head offices

"There were days when there were TV crews at the end of the drive"

There were days when there were TV crews at the end of the drive. We'd say, 'Listen, do you want to go out the back way?' And she'd say, 'To be honest, they're going to hound us until they've got the picture. So why don't I just go, get the picture done, and then they'll leave us alone.' I thought she was very mature for a 26-year-old, and I think she's been quite good at neither courting the press nor sticking two fingers in the air at them. I don't think I would have been so polite."

It was agreed that she would work three days a week. As an assistant accessories buyer, Kate's role would have involved working with the buyer to decide what items Jigsaw stocked. According to *Blackwell's Fashion Buying*, "A good buyer needs stamina but should also be enthusiastic, conscientious, professional, decisive, numerate, creative, imaginative and well-motivated. To succeed in this career, buyers need to have foresight and develop skills in people management and time management." According to Belle, Kate certainly had all of these skills. "She sat in the kitchen at lunchtime and chatted with everyone from the van drivers to the accounts girls. She wasn't precious. A lot of people have distorted it to say we're friends with her parents but I've only met them four times."

Kate left the job in November 2007, stating that she wanted some time to herself as a result of all the pressures of the relationship with Prince William. Her next move was to begin working for her parents' company Party Pieces, a place she knew she could always fall back on while she found her feet. Party Pieces was founded in 1987, when Carole Middleton decided to quit her job as an air hostess for British Airways. She was living in Jordan at the time, with Kate's father Michael who was a flight dispatcher, also working for BA. Carole had decided the time was right to return to England to ensure her children received the best education. The company she founded specialises in partyware, such as personalised cakes and balloons for children, as well as for adults. This was a time when there was very little available on the high street for hosting parties. It soon went from strength to strength. After the inevitable struggles of the Covid-19 pandemic however, the business went into administration in 2023.

All three of Carole Middleton's children – Pippa, James and Kate – worked on the business at some point. Kate worked on the marketing side of the company – handily the company has its own marketing and buying team, so her experience at Jigsaw had by no means gone to waste. According to the company website, Kate was responsible for starting the 1st birthday party section of the company.

After leaving Jigsaw, Kate also turned her hand to photography. She took some photographs for the Party Pieces website and was then able to use a valuable connection from her university days – the photographer Alistair Morrison – to arrange and curate an exhibition of his photography at the prestigious Bluebird restaurant in Chelsea. His photographs included portraits of A-list celebrities, including Tom Cruise, Kate Winslet, Catherine Zeta-Jones and Sting.

BOTTOM LEFT The Middleton's family business, Party Pieces, specialised in children's birthday parties. Here their website stocks a 'New Little Prince' range in celebration of the birth of their grandson, Prince George, in 2013

BOTTOM RIGHT Kate at the Bluebird event, curating photography for her friend from university, Alistair Morrison

Towards the end of the 2000s it soon became clear that Kate's relationship with William, despite their brief hiatus, was becoming increasingly more serious. However, this took its toll on Kate's career. Their relationship not only made it almost impossible for Kate to hold down any kind of job because of the intense press intrusion, but it also made it seem more likely that she would become a full-time member of the royal family and a future queen. Kate had to mould herself into the role, becoming more careful about her image. She also had to make sure that she could trust those around her not to compromise her. The family business, then, was the perfect environment for her to continue to work until news broke of her engagement to Prince William in November 2010 and her future role was secured. She left the business in January 2011, four months before her wedding day.

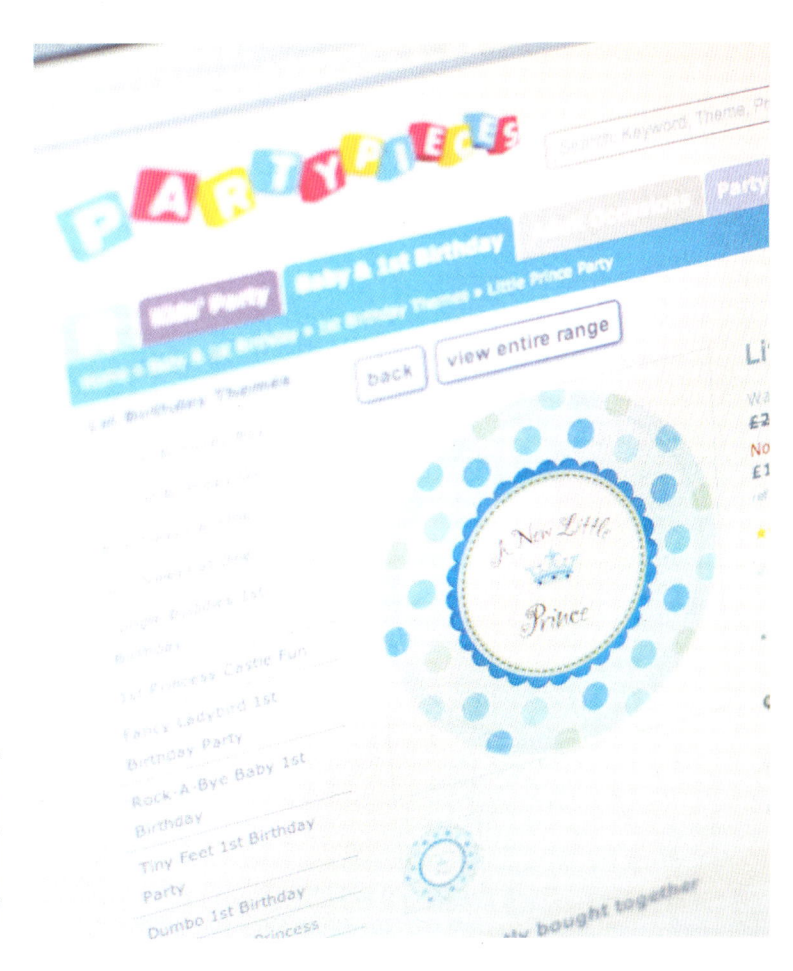

Images: Getty & Alamy

Caring KATE'S CAUSES and CHARITIES

The Princess of Wales has given her support a range of causes. Mental health, care for seriously ill children and tackling social stigmas are some of the causes Kate has taken under her wing. Her understanding of modern life and its difficulties has allowed her to establish her own place in the royal family and help charities close to her heart

On World Mental Health Day in 2017, the then Duke of Cambridge revealed that one of the most high-profile and successful royal campaigns of recent times had all been down to Kate. Talking about the Heads Together project, which had made mental health a national talking point and brought help to tens of thousands of people, William said, "It was Catherine who... had seen that at the core of adult issues like addiction and family breakdown, unresolved childhood mental health issues were often part of the problem". It was the culmination of several years of work by Kate who, from the very earliest days of her marriage, had given her backing to organisations and projects focused on some of the most difficult issues in modern society.

That began with the very first patronages she took on. In January 2012, it was confirmed that Catherine had chosen to give her official backing to a range of organisations, including some that touched on issues she had already shown were very close to her heart.

Action on Addiction was one of the organisations that now counted Kate as one of its patrons. The organisation aims to counter addiction to drugs and alcohol through support networks and by using the best possible research to discover the causes of dependency. Working in the community and at special rehabilitation centres, it reaches out to thousands of people every year. Kate made her first visit to the charity as its patron in February 2012 when she visited two of its facilities in a matter of weeks. It was a tough and gritty issue for the new royal to tackle, but she showed how important it was to her as she discussed many of the problems faced by addicts and those who help them in her engagements for the charity.

Kate's desire to help children was also seen in her first raft of patronages. She gave her support to The Art Room, a charity in Oxfordshire that helps children to re-engage with life after trauma by using painting, drawing and visual stimulation. Two visits to the charity quickly followed and in the summer after she became its patron, Kate also attended a gala

RIGHT Supporting causes that help children, like this city farm, have been a priority for the Princess since she began her public life in 2011. Many of her patronages involve charities for young people, with a focus on tackling problems as early as possible

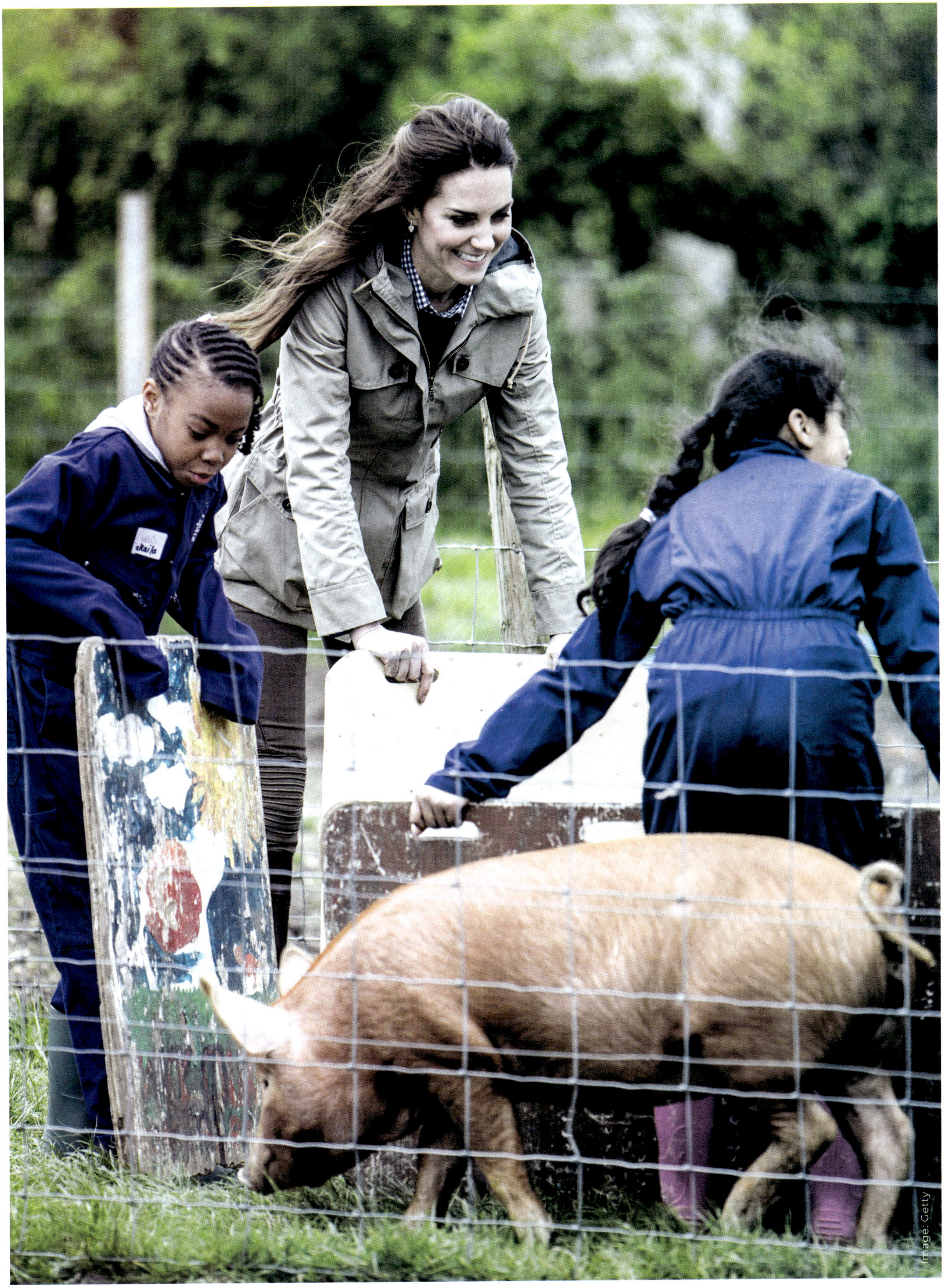

Image: Getty

theatre fundraiser for The Art Room, which went from local concern to national fame in weeks thanks to her input. On top of this, the new Duchess also embraced the poignant and often overlooked area of children's palliative care, becoming patron of the East Anglia Children's Hospices. Kate would give her first public speech in support of this particular organisation and has paid private visits to its buildings as well as carrying out a series of high-profile public engagements and giving her support to its campaigns, including one called 'The Nook', which aims to set up a brand-new children's hospice amid the calm woods of Norfolk.

At the same time, she announced that she would become a volunteer with the Scout Association. She is now its joint president, alongside the Duke of Kent. She became involved in another well-supported cause a year later when she was named as a patron of the 100 Women in Finance Initiative, which aims to help female entrepreneurs succeed. She joined as a patron of the organisation that counted the then Countess of Wessex as a Global Ambassador.

By then, Kate was expecting her first baby and while a new family life was beginning to take shape, so was her nascent interest in children's mental health. While still pregnant with George, she became the patron of Place2Be, which provides emotional support for pupils at schools across the country. It had grown from a small organisation supporting five educational establishments to one involving over 280, and Kate would go on to visit many of the schools it helps, as well as taking part in major conferences organised by the charity to debate and investigate mental health issues in children.

Another of the organisations taken under the Cambridge wing in 2013 would have a starring role in one of Kate's first post-baby appearances. In April of that year, Kate became patron of SportsAid, which aims to support the rising stars in all sports as they begin their attempts to excel. Less than two months after giving birth to Prince George, Kate visited one of its initiatives at the Copper Box in east London, taking to the court for a spot of sport, which showed just how flat her tummy already was so soon after pregnancy. The images ensured maximum publicity for the charity, ensuring the Princess put her new cause on the front of just about every newspaper, helping them as much as she possibly could.

In fact, sport was to become a major theme of Kate's work over the coming years. In 2014, she became involved with the 1851 Trust, which endeavours to inspire young people from all walks of life to take up sailing. It also aims to use sport to help children develop skills in science, technology and engineering. Kate has been a keen yachtsman since an early age and her involvement in the charity has also allowed her to give her support to teams entering the Americas Cup.

Tennis is another great passion of Kate's, and from the early years of her marriage, she has been a regular at Wimbledon, cheering on home-grown talents like Andy Murray, as well as encouraging a new generation to enjoy the sport. When the late Queen started to pass on some of her patronages following her 90th birthday, it seemed

ABOVE The Heads Together campaign was announced to the world in April 2016 with Kate joining her husband and brother-in-law in a campaign to get the initiative noticed

> "As a History of Art graduate, it was inevitable she would take on patronages in the arts world"

all but inevitable that Catherine would take on the role formerly held by the monarch at the All England Lawn Tennis and Croquet Club. Elizabeth II had been patron for decades, but stepped aside in 2017 when the baton was passed to Kate. Since then her involvement with the club – and, in particular, the famous tournament played there every summer – has increased. In 2018, she invited her new sister-in-law, Meghan Markle, to tour Wimbledon with her, where they met staff, coaches and some of the ballgirls and boys who keep the tournament going every year.

At the same time as she became patron of the home of Wimbledon, Kate took on an equally important role within the tennis world, again following the decision of the late Queen to stand aside. She became patron of the Lawn Tennis Association in 2017, supporting its work to promote the sport through providing training and facilities. She shares royal responsibilities at the organisation with the Duchess of Gloucester, who is its honorary president.

As a History of Art graduate, it was perhaps inevitable that Kate would end up taking on a wide range of patronages in the arts world. One of the first organisations to win her formal support was the National Portrait Gallery. Since becoming its patron in 2012, she attended a number of glittering galas to support its work and promote exhibitions. It was also the setting for an event starring Kate herself. The then Duchess of Cambridge posed for Vogue in 2016 to mark its centenary and some of the images taken played a starring role in a special exhibition about the magazine at the gallery that summer.

Noticeably, Kate's later arts patronages have been centred on museums as popular with younger visitors as grown ups, perhaps an indication of how her outlook has changed since she had children. In 2014, she became patron of the Natural History Museum, close to her home at the time at Kensington Palace, while in 2018, she was named as the first royal patron of another local landmark, the Victoria and Albert Museum. Her work with both institutions saw her support a wide range of learning and creative initiatives while she was also on hand to bid farewell to Dippy, the dinosaur skeleton that had famously stood in the Natural History's main atrium for years. She's already started to introduce her children to her causes, with Prince George, Princess Charlotte and Prince Louis snapped visiting museums with their mum.

It was soon after the birth of Princess Charlotte that Kate's most famous initiative first started taking shape. The Heads Together project, bringing together charities and organisations supporting those with a wide range of mental health problems, was formally launched in May 2016, but had been in the planning for many months before that. As Prince William said proudly, his wife had realised that the couple, along with Prince Harry, were all working with organisations that had mental health as one of their main focal points and she began to think of ways to bring their work together to create a bigger impact.

The campaign was first announced in the spring of 2016 when the organisers of the London Marathon confirmed that Heads Together would be the official charity of the 2017 race. Kate, along with William and Harry, then spoke about their idea while posing in headbands to promote the initiative. At the official launch in London, the Duchess explained her motivation for beginning the project, explaining, "Too often people feel afraid to admit that they are struggling with their mental health. This fear of judgement stops people from getting the help they need, which can destroy families and end lives".

The royals explained that they wanted Heads Together to "change the conversation on mental health"

ABOVE As patron of the National Portrait Gallery, Kate is used to exhibitions but in 2016 she came face to face with herself during one engagement in support of her cause

"Kate has always been keen to include causes close to her heart on the many overseas visits she has made in her royal career"

and to get people to open up about their problems. The campaign initially involved seven charities: Best Beginnings, CALM, Contact, The Mix, Mind, Young Minds and Place2Be, whose work was already so familiar to its patron.

Kate then took the lead in promoting the campaign. Over the coming months she sat the forefront of a string of high-profile public events to support the initiative, including a visit to Young Minds where she donned a headset to listen to how advisers talk to parents calling their helpline when they're worried about a child. She also guest edited the *Huffington Post* for a day, inviting journalists into her home to help her put together a series of articles outlining the issues and possible solutions. In October 2016, Kate gave another speech in support of Heads Together on World Mental Health Day, saying "I feel it is our duty to do what we can... to shine a spotlight on emotional wellbeing. But first... we must tackle the stigma that stops people asking for help in the first place."

The Princess was also at the forefront of events marking Heads Together's special place at the London Marathon. In the days before the event, she went out and about to unveil some of the postboxes that had been decorated with special headbands for the event, while she also took a lead role in the very personal and open videos made by the royal trio where they talked about mental health in the hope it would encourage others to do the same.

Catherine was also on hand to cheer runners over the finish line as thousands raced to raise funds for and awareness of the campaign that she had done so much to steer to success.

Kate has always been keen to include causes close to her heart on the many overseas visits she has made in her royal career. On one of her first major tours, to Australia in 2014, she asked for engagements at children's hospices to be included on the itinerary at a

LEFT The Princess of Wales has been a hands-on patron for many of her charities, often taking to the water in support of the 1851 Trust

time when palliative care for young people was under-resourced. Mental health initiatives were under focus on visits to Canada in 2014.

The Prince and Princess of Wales have become well-known for their sporting competitiveness while on tour, whether it's racing yachts round Auckland Harbour during a stay in New Zealand, trying their luck at archery while in Bhutan or having a go at ice hockey on a recent stay in Sweden. The events are always used to underline the impact that sport can have on both physical and emotional wellbeing. Since her marriage, Kate has been a Principal Patron of the Royal Foundation, which develops programmes and projects based on the interests of Kate and William, and formerly Harry and Meghan. It does this by bringing together organisations with a track record in the area of concern and it was through the Foundation that Kate launched a steering group to look at the topic of

children's mental health. The Princess asked them to formulate ideas for improving emotional wellbeing among the under fives and the Royal Foundation then worked to find a way to put that into practice.

It's an area that is coming to dominate her work. In 2016 she also became patron of the children's mental health charity The Anna Freud Centre, and in 2017 she added Action for Children, which provides support and care for vulnerable children, to her list of charities.

It all means that we can expect more projects in this area, and others, from Kate in the very near future. Her past record shows that she will be determined to make it a success, to keep on providing the strong support she has given, so far, to all the charities and causes she has become involved with. With the death of the Queen many of the royal family's patronages shifted around, but Kate can always be relied upon to support many causes.

RIGHT Kate's love of children and the issues that affect them has been clear throughout her royal career

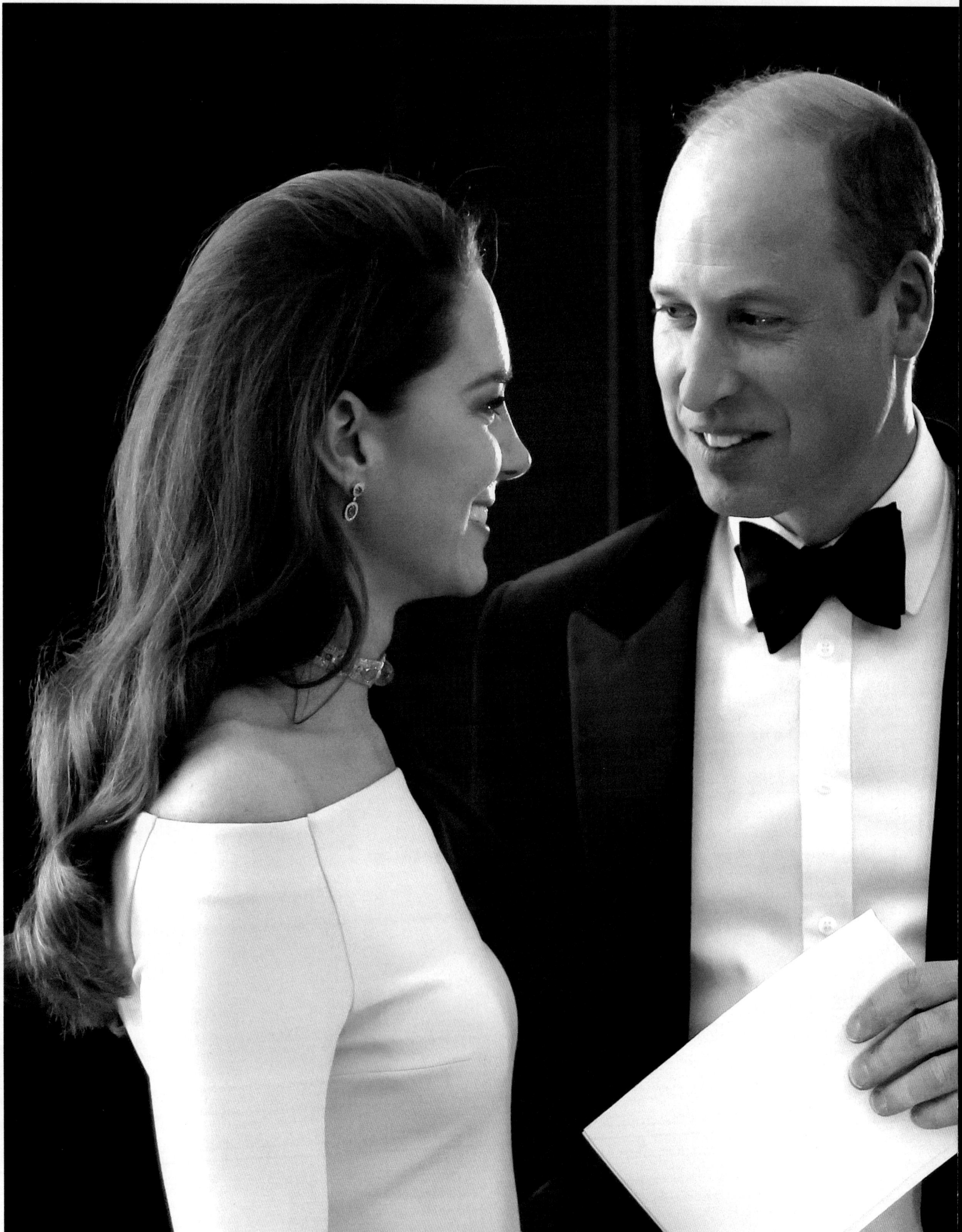

WILL & KATE
The Royal Couple

082 .... The Prince and the Commoner
094 .... William and Kate's Royal Wedding
104 .... The In-Laws
110 .... Keeping Up with the Cambridges
122 .... Modernising the Monarchy

The PRINCE and the COMMONER

Now firmly considered to be one of the Windsor dynasty's most-loved couples by people from every corner of the globe, the Prince and Princess of Wales's romance began rather inauspiciously in their university years, much like many other modern relationships

Cool, calm and collected was not the way to describe Catherine Elizabeth Middleton the first time she met her future husband. Having been nicknamed a 'princess in waiting' at school for having a poster of Prince William on her bedroom wall, when she was introduced to him at university she apparently went bright red and shyly scuttled off.

In 2001, Prince William called St Salvator's Hall home at the University of St Andrews. Just a few rooms away was the woman who would help shape the rest of his life: Kate. As coursemates and housemates, their friendship blossomed throughout their first year, and Kate became a calming influence on him. She was even credited with helping to convince him to stay at the end of their first year when he began having doubts. However, it quickly turned into something more for William.

William's attitude towards his shy, sporty friend changed at a charity fashion show held at the university in March 2002. After paying £200 for a front-row seat, he was apparently stunned when he saw her strutting down the catwalk in a see-through black dress. He leaned over to his friend next to him and whispered, "Wow, Kate's hot!" But it wouldn't be that easy for him – Kate was in a relationship and just wasn't interested.

However, that didn't stop them from moving in together in their second year, along with two other friends. Their second-year home saw was a terraced Georgian house in St Andrews, while their home in the third year – with the same set of friends – was a cottage just outside the town. But there was good news for William early in 2003 when Kate split from her boyfriend. Could he win over his housemate?

In 2004, it was confirmed by a single picture taken at Klosters, a Swiss ski resort: William and Kate were in a relationship. With the news breaking, what the world didn't know was that they had been seeing each other since Christmas. They had managed to avoid the inevitable until that point by never leaving their house together, and arriving at social engagements separately. It was a crushing realisation that the safety and security of the media blackout at St Andrews had ended. Now their relationship was there for the world to see.

Following their graduation, the real world awaited them. Their love story had been almost idyllic from the moment they fell for one another as young university students, but away from the St Andrews bubble, Kate and William were quickly reminded of how different life would be as they moved away from its sheltered walls. Suddenly

RIGHT Kate and William began building a shared life together soon after falling in love at university. They enjoyed each other's interests, like the rugby they are seen watching together here, and were regularly seen together. The romance would lead to the altar

Image: Getty

LEFT During her break with William, Kate became part of the Sisterhood Cross Channel Challenge Team and was often seen out training with them

LEFT By early 2005, the serious nature of her relationship with William was clear when Kate was asked to join a skiing holiday with her boyfriend and his family

they found themselves exposed to a new level of scrutiny as their romance became public property. However serious they felt about one another, the strains of so much interest would take their toll. Thankfully, the couple's love only grew stronger as they negotiated their own path from college romance to royal wedding.

The initial months of their courtship after St Andrews were relatively easy, while providing a taste of the challenges yet to come. They enjoyed their graduation day together and after the press interest at the university itself, they were finally able to relax with friends and family at the private celebrations afterwards. But even then both were exceptionally aware of the attention that they so easily attracted and had learned to trust only their closest friends and family with news of their relationship.

However, William was now expected to take on more royal duties and in the summer of 2005 he headed to New Zealand to represent the Queen, then spent some time in his beloved Kenya. Although Kate was able to join him there briefly, more work beckoned for William in the autumn of that year. His future included the challenge of running huge estates, firstly when he became heir to the throne and then, ultimately, as the monarch himself. He was sent off to learn the ropes at Chatsworth, home of the Dukes of Devonshire, who had long been friendly with the royal family.

It was the first of several teaching experiences lined up for the young prince and which kept him busy while his girlfriend settled into a quieter life. William had to be seen to be busy; there was a public expectation that he would fill more and more of his time with royal duties. Among those responsibilities lay marriage and children. As his relationship with Kate seemed to weather the storm that leaving university can inflict on so many romances that start at college, her name was mentioned more and more as that of a future queen.

However, William barely had time to see his girlfriend, let alone plan a wedding. For centuries, royal princes had been expected to have military training and expertise and as 2005 came to an end, it was announced that the second-in-line to the throne would follow his little brother, Harry, to the officer training college at Sandhurst. While William embarked on his first round of military training at the Royal Military Academy Sandhurst, Kate began work as a party planner at Party Pieces, the company owned by her parents, Michael and Carole Middleton. The regime was tough, especially in the initial months, and would leave little time for romance. The relationship was long-distance – William couldn't leave Sandhurst during his training and Kate was busy in London – but the couple made it work. Ahead of starting at the college, in January 2006 William whisked Kate away for a skiing holiday, but soon she found herself alone again.

After leaving university, she spent her time between her parents' home in Bucklebury, Berkshire and London, where they had a small flat. However, with William away from the public gaze, Kate became the focal point of their relationship and came in for some criticism after being seen at a string of parties and nights out. What might be seen as run-of-the-mill behaviour for a young woman from a well-off family became a matter of national debate, as commentators asked whether this was the behaviour of a queen-in-waiting. Kate was caught in a difficult position – her relationship appeared to be for the long term, but without any official status she was fast becoming tabloid fodder and there was little she could do about it.

In 2006, the couple appeared together at a family wedding. Although Kate hadn't attended the wedding of Prince Charles and Camilla Parker-Bowles with William, they were both present at the ceremony of Camilla's daughter, Laura, and Harry Lopes. Avid royal watchers saw Kate's appearance as a sign that she was preparing to be a permanent fixture in Prince William's life, and they had more reason to say that in July when she went to cheer on William and his brother at a polo event with Harry's then-girlfriend, Chelsy Davy. And while Kate and William followed royal etiquette in public with very few displays of affection, behind closed doors they apparently called each other 'Babykins' and 'Big Willie'.

She took another step towards royal life in December 2006, when she attended William's passing out parade at Sandhurst with her parents. The arrival of William's girlfriend caused huge excitement, especially as the event was overseen by the Queen. The Duke of Edinburgh, the Prince of Wales and the Duchess of Cornwall were all also present, and the sight of the whole Middleton family next to the royals seemed to add an air of inevitability to the prospect of William and Kate finally marrying. Although Kate and her parents didn't sit with the senior royals in attendance – Prince Charles, Prince Philip and, of course, the Queen herself – the fact that she was there and accompanied by the Prince of Wales's chief of staff, Prince William's private secretary and his diary secretary, only fuelled rumours that a royal engagement was definitely on the horizon. Some shops even began producing wedding souvenirs in what was clearly a publicity-seeking exercise, but it reminded the young couple – as if they needed telling – that their love story was very far from being a personal affair.

> *"The initial months of their courtship after St Andrews were relatively easy."*

LEFT Kate photographed while attending the wedding of Laura Parker Bowles and Harry Lopes in May 2006

"Both were wary of the attention they attracted and had learned to trust only closest friends and family with news of their relationship"

That became abundantly clear just weeks later when Kate was surrounded by paparazzi as she left her London flat on her 25th birthday. Many had decided that this moment would coincide with an engagement announcement and Kate was barely able to get down the street as photographers surrounded her. William was furious, quickly issuing a statement demanding for the media harassment of his girlfriend to stop and describing the events as "unbearable for all concerned".

The intervention provided a brief respite, but Kate was finding out that even with Palace support, the scrutiny into her every move continued. She was then working as an assistant buyer for fashion chain, Jigsaw, but when that came to an end she returned to supporting her family's company, Party Pieces. This aroused ongoing debate in certain parts of the media, with some commentators questioning whether she really worked at all and others calling her choice an easy option. She soon realised that once more, she had no way of taking on her critics. All she could do was grin and bear it.

A tougher challenge had also now presented itself. Soon after Kate and William were seen looking less than happy in each other's company at the Cheltenham Festival in March 2007, it was announced that the couple had decided to part company. Kate retreated to the safety of her family home, where her mother, Carole Middleton, was on hand to offer comfort and advice. William, meanwhile, was spotted at nightclubs in the days surrounding the split. But his former girlfriend proved she was more than able to match him at his own game and was soon seen out and about herself, enjoying her single status with her younger sister, Pippa, at her side.

However, hopes of them getting back together were dashed in 2007. In April, sources reported that William and Kate had parted ways mutually and amicably, with media attention

ABOVE Kate and William's appearance at the Cheltenham Festival in March 2007 came just weeks before it was confirmed they had split

LEFT Kate and William made their first formal appearance together in April 2008, when the Prince received his RAF Wings

being a major contributing factor. Kate certainly hadn't been enjoying the paparazzi presence and it had only been increasing. It was hard to forget her 25th birthday, when she'd opened her door to a wall of photographers.

While Clarence House declined to comment at the time of the split, William later said: "We were both very young... and we were both defining ourselves... it was just a bit of space". The press and the distance had got to both of them. Possibly aware of the paparazzi presence that wasn't going to go away, Kate made the effort to keep herself busy. She went to Ireland with her mother, spent some time in Ibiza, and had fun nights out in London with Pippa. When she wasn't enjoying herself on the social scene, she was waking up at 6.30am to do rigorous rowing training.

William apparently kept calling Kate after they parted ways. The future princess chose to ignore the incessant ringing of her phone, but proved herself to be independent and loyal. She was getting on with life and steadfastly refusing to talk to the press about the relationship.

As the summer of 2007 dawned, Kate also joined 'The Sisterhood', an all-female team who planned to cross the English Channel in a dragon boat to raise money for charity. Soon, the sight of Kate attending early-morning training sessions and enjoying life with her team were splashed all over the papers. William was among the first to notice and, realising that he had made a big mistake in ending their relationship, began to make contact with his former flame once more.

To the world's delight, the split didn't last. In fact, at the Concert for Diana on 1 July 2007, it seemed like the relationship was on the mend, as Kate took her place in the royal box at Wembley Stadium, albeit a few rows behind William. The day before, he had been asked by a journalist if Kate was likely to attend, and he graciously responded: "I've got lots of friends coming. Everyone's going to be there

ABOVE Kate attended the Concert for Diana, organised by William and Harry, in July 2007. It was the first real public indication that her royal relationship was possibly getting back on track

"Sources reported that William and Kate had parted ways mutually and amicably"

on the night and it's going to be a very good night." His brother cheekily quipped: "Really well avoided, William, very diplomatic".

In August, Britain's best-loved couple were off to the Seychelles for a romantic holiday. To keep the trip low-key, they reportedly booked the entire resort at a cost of £20,000 and checked in under the pseudonyms of Martin and Rosemary. Speculation about an engagement reached fever pitch and rumours were growing that Kate had been given the keys to Clarence House, William's official residence. However, those hoping for a royal wedding were sorely disappointed.

Easter 2008 saw the couple return to Klosters for more skiing to celebrate the end of William's intensive pilot training course at RAF Cranwell in Lincolnshire. For the first time, Kate was granted a royal protection officer, and when Prince Charles, as he was then, joined them later it was a sign that Kate had well and truly been welcomed into the fold. The following month, Kate was present when William received his wings, qualifying as a fully trained pilot.

In June 2008, it seemed as though Kate was being pulled deeper into the royal family. She attended the wedding of Peter Phillips, William's cousin, alone as her boyfriend was duty-bound to an event, and later that month attended the ceremony for William becoming the 1,000th Royal Knight of the Garter at Windsor Castle.

Over time, Kate was dubbed 'Waity Katie' by the British press, who were wondering why William was taking so long to get down on one knee. Despite the small break in 2007, they had been together since the end of 2003, and the longer they waited, the more excited the media became.

What possibly didn't help the rumours were reports emerging in 2009 that the Queen had invited Kate for an audience at Balmoral over the August bank holiday. A royal source claimed that Queen Elizabeth was planning on discussing how things would change should William ask for her hand in marriage – the clearest of signals that Kate was being prepared for entering the royal family.

Pressure mounting about an engagement, the couple carried out their duties and lived their lives ignoring the press. In June 2010, they moved into a four-bedroom farmhouse in north Wales close to RAF Valley in Anglesey, the base where William was to be stationed for the next three years. Things became relatively quiet and they could enjoy their rural Welsh life.

But the press didn't relent. When William and Kate were pictured at

LEFT When the couple attended a friend's wedding in Gloucestershire in October 2010, they were hiding a secret – their own engagement, which had taken place in Africa weeks earlier

a friend's wedding in October that year in Gloucestershire, all anyone could notice was how in love the two of them looked – more than they had ever looked before, at least in public. What no one knew was that they had a secret. William had taken his mother's engagement ring on their trip to Kenya not long before. One night under the stars he got down on one knee – and Kate had said yes.

The news the world had been waiting for finally came on the morning of 16 November 2010, in a brief statement from Clarence House. Apparently the Queen only heard about it a few hours before. The official communication revealed that Prince William had asked Kate's father, Michael Middleton, for permission to propose and added that Prince Charles was "delighted" by the engagement. The announcement dominated the news, with early editions of papers rushed to the stands in the UK and TV channels switching schedules to all-day coverage of this milestone moment of this royal romance.

Just hours after the engagement was confirmed, the couple appeared before the press in the grand settings of the State Apartments of St. James' Palace in London. And when Kate stepped out to face the photographers, she had a very special ring to show off. On the third finger of her left hand was the sapphire and diamond engagement ring that had once belonged to Diana, Princess of Wales.

The jewel was already one of the most famous royal gems in the world by the time that Prince William presented it to his fiancée. In the aftermath of her death, the princes had been allowed to choose a keepsake from their mother's most precious possessions. The ring had been the pick of Prince Harry. However, when William decided to propose to Kate, he asked his brother if he might use the ring for this special question. They then both agreed that the ring had to be used for this royal engagement. Speaking after his marriage plans had been announced, the groom-to-be revealed that it was his way of making sure that his mother didn't miss out on his wedding.

The 18-carat gold band of the ring, featuring a 12-carat Ceylon sapphire surrounded by 14 brilliant-cut diamonds, had to be altered to fit Kate's finger. Jewellers made it smaller by placing platinum beads inside the ring's band. And while its first appearance as a royal engagement ring had caused some comment because Diana had chosen it from a catalogue from royal jewellers Garrards, William's decision to present it to Kate was widely applauded.

Kate also paid tribute to her fiancé's late mother with her choice of outfit for the engagement call. Diana, as a nervous 19-year-old bride-to-be, had headed into London and picked up an off-the-peg suit in bright blue to match the stone in her engagement ring. Kate Middleton had done exactly the same. She made her first official royal appearance in a deep blue dress by Issa that had been bought on a shopping trip. It was a sweet nod to Diana and an instant fashion hit. Within hours the dress, later known as 'The Kate', had not only sold out but also boosted the profile and profits of this small fashion label immeasurably.

The couple were clearly nervous for this big appearance, walking into the huge room in single file before standing in front of a fireplace and linking arms. But their anxieties were understandable. Before them loomed a huge bank of camera lenses as media from around the world jostled for the photo they had craved for so long: William and Kate as an engaged couple. Once the couple finally began to relax, they started to exchange glances. Their smiles widened and it was clear that as well as being a future king and queen consort, they were first and foremost the young couple who had fallen in love at the University of St Andrews.

Soon after facing the cameras, they sat down for an exclusive interview with ITV's Tom Bradby, with William referencing the nerves they both felt.

89

He said they were "like sort of ducks, very calm on the surface with little feet going under the water," but both confirmed they were very excited by the changes and had been talking about getting married for "a long time". However, Kate said she hadn't seen William's proposal coming, saying "it was a total shock when it came".

The couple were pressed for details of the proposal. Kate described the experience as "romantic, there's a true romantic in there". Asked why he had chosen his late mother's engagement ring for his future wife, the Prince explained "obviously she's not going to be around to share any of the fun and excitement of it all – this was my way of keeping her close to it all."

The interview was also an opportunity for the couple to finally share some details of the courtship that had fascinated the world for so long, but which had been as private as it could be. William explained that they had quickly struck up a rapport after their first meeting at St Andrews, while Kate confessed to "going bright red" when first introduced to him before becoming "very close friends from quite early on". And the future king admitted that "when I first met Kate, I knew there was something very special about her".

They also addressed the split, which had become such a well-known part of their relationship, with the bride-to-be admitting "at the time I wasn't very happy about it but actually it made me a stronger person". The couple were keen to look to the future, with Kate outlining how she wanted to try and make a difference in the new, high-profile role she was about to take on.

Although the couple had been followed for much of their relationship, it was nothing like the scrutiny they now faced as their courtship moved into the more serious and formal stage of marriage preparations. They embarked on a tour of the UK, visiting all four parts of the country in a series of engagements. One of their first official public appearances was at the University of St Andrews, where they had first fallen in love. On the tour, they showed their fresh take on royal life and the sense of humour that had brought them together by taking part in a pancake race in their visit to Belfast.

Kate also got her first taste of the traditions that were waiting for her after marriage. In the early part of 2011, she launched her first boat on a visit to Anglesey, while she impressed many by singing the Welsh national anthem in Welsh. Wherever they went, the young couple were greeted by huge crowds as their popularity grew and grew in the run up to the wedding.

Behind the scenes, Kate was putting the finishing touches to the big day. She was also confirmed into the Church of England in this last part of her courtship, ready to take her place at the side of the man who would one day be its Supreme Head.

As all the final preparations for the marriage were being made, the Queen issued an Instrument of Consent, which gave her permission for William and Kate's union. Written on vellum with intricate calligraphy beautifully decorated in symbolic images, it declared: "We have consented... to the contracting of matrimony between Our Most Dearly Beloved Grandson... and Our Trusty and Well Beloved Catherine Elizabeth Middleton".

Trusty and well beloved is an ancient term typically used for royal subjects with no title of their own, but in many ways it perfectly summed up the place that Kate had won for herself in the affections of the House of Windsor during her courtship.

She'd had time to get to know her future husband and his family, and in turn they had the chance to come to appreciate Kate's devotion to William and to the life that she would now inhabit. It was a very royal happy ending and the perfect beginning to one of the most important regal marriages of the 21st century.

RIGHT The future of the monarchy is bright and hopeful as the family faces big changes in its dynamics in the upcoming years

BELOW Kate's sapphire engagement ring previously belong to Diana. William said that giving the ring to Kate was his way of making sure his mother didn't miss out on his wedding day

> "William had his mother's engagement ring in his rucksack on their trip to Kenya"

"Behind the scenes, Kate was putting the finishing touches to the big day that had seemed to be in the offing for so long"

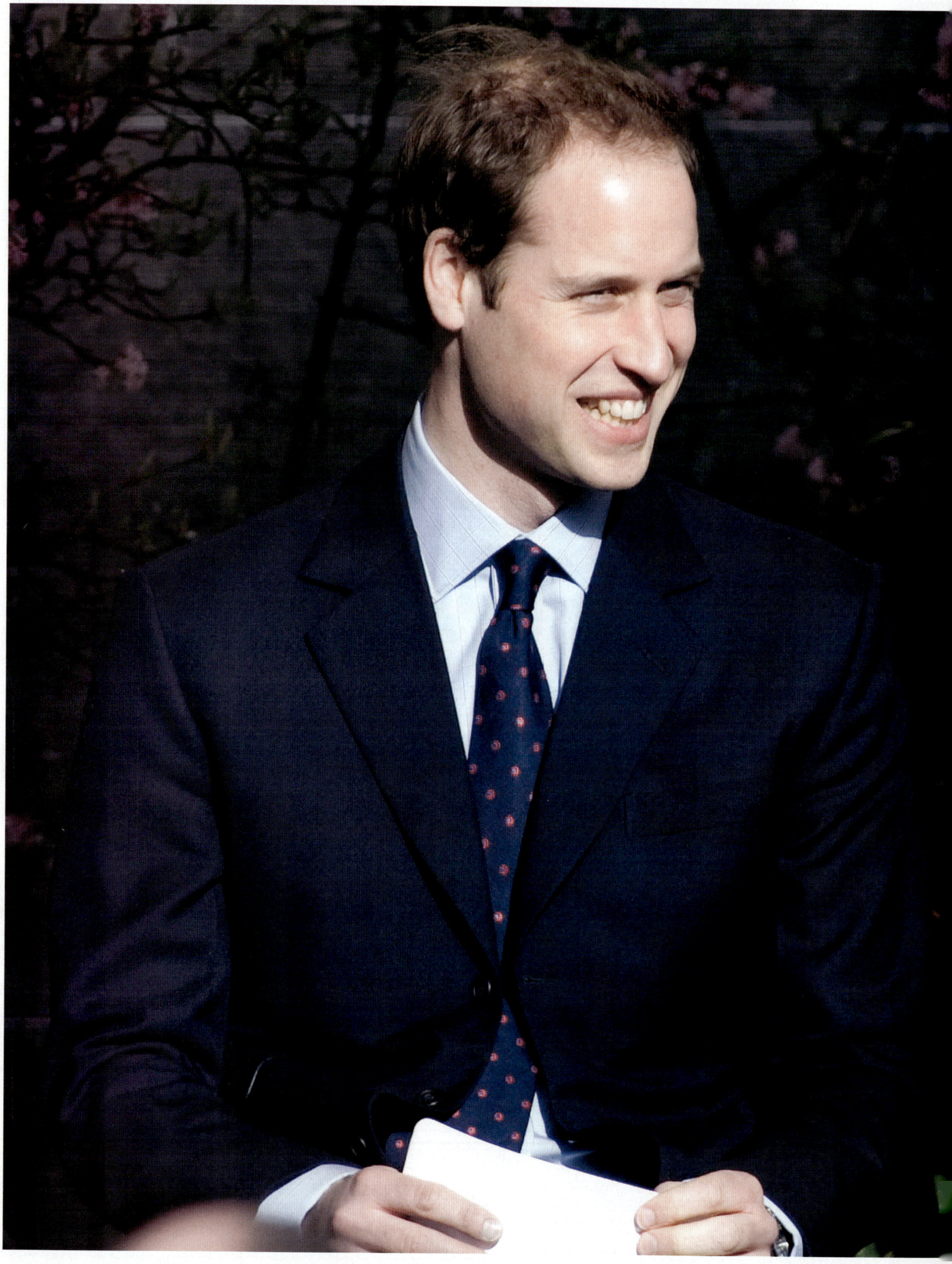

Despite all the pageantry and pomp that can surround them, it's easy to see the young couple that fell in love at university

WILLIAM and KATE'S ROYAL WEDDING

It was the royal wedding that the world had been waiting for as the second in line to the throne married the love of his life – and everyone got to watch

We're supposed to have just a small family affair." Prince William's joke to his father-in-law, Michael Middleton, as they stood before the Archbishop of Canterbury on 29 April 2011 summed up the spirit of this very modern royal wedding. While William's bride, Kate, would be in line for a consort's crown as soon as they were pronounced husband and wife, she had planned her special day to be as family-oriented as possible. The result was one of the most magical royal weddings of recent times.

Kate had managed to keep many of her wedding ideas under wraps, no mean feat considering the global interest that had been shown in every aspect of the marriage ever since the couple had announced their engagement. The date was announced just before Christmas, around the same time that the Queen gave her consent to the day being a public holiday. However, the names of dress designer, bridesmaids and details of the bride's wedding attire were all secret. It only served to stoke interest further.

One of the few early details to emerge came as no surprise. The couple decided to marry at Westminster Abbey, a popular wedding venue for the House of Windsor for almost a century. Kate would follow in the footsteps of the Queen and the Queen Mother, who had both been royal brides in this ancient church. However, she would be the first woman to marry a son of a Prince of Wales there. Despite the 20th century vogue for royal weddings at Westminster, it had actually been spurned as a regal marriage venue for almost

RIGHT As the bells of Westminster Abbey rang and the crowds cheered, Kate and William walked out into the April sunshine, appearing for the first time as Duke and Duchess of Cambridge

six centuries. Kate would be the first commoner to wed a royal inside its hallowed walls.

But while the world was kept waiting for news of the wedding, behind palace doors Kate was in complete control. She planned every detail and, aware of the pressure she was under, even hired a voice coach to help her sound confident as she spoke her vows. Anthony Gordon Lennox taught the bride how to control her voice and breathe effectively to calm her nerves so that she was word perfect on the day.

Kate's dream was to create a wedding that had the feel of an English country celebration. However, the bride knew that the splendour of a royal marriage had to be included in that. The regal side of the celebrations was clear from the invitations, which were sent out in the name of the Queen in the middle of February. The 1,900 guests asked to attend the ceremony at the Abbey received heavily embossed cards, featuring the monarch's royal cipher at the top, and informing them that the

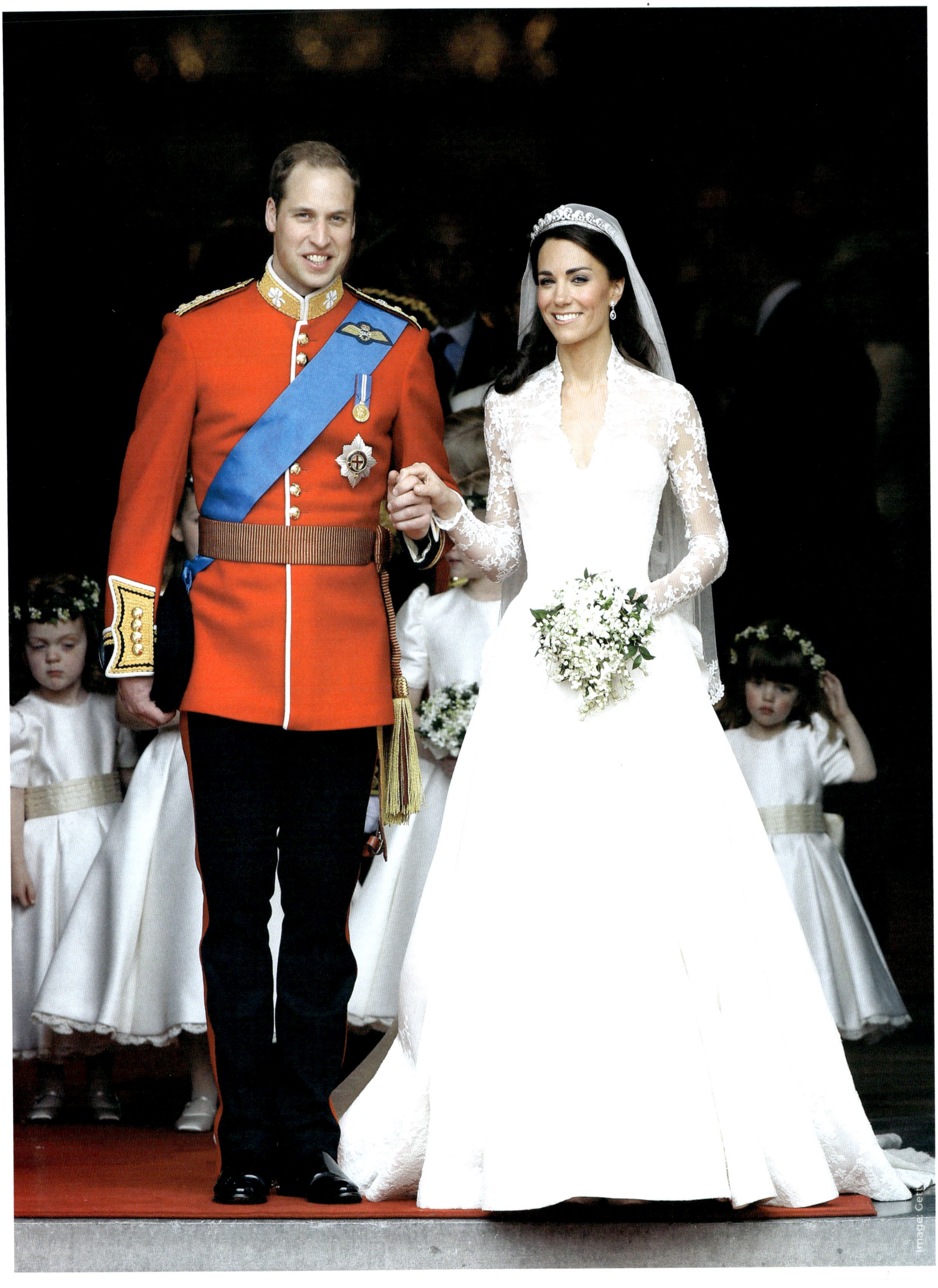
Image: Gett

'Lord Chamberlain is commanded by the Queen' to issue them with an invitation. Responses had to be sent by post to the Lord Chamberlain's Office. When he had initially drafted the guest list, William had told his grandmother that he didn't know any of the 600-plus people that he apparently had to invite. Queen Elizabeth reportedly tore up the list and told her grandson to figure out who it was that he and Kate wanted to be there and they'd worry about all of the dignitaries and formalities later.

Among those on the list were royals from across Europe. While William and Kate filled over half the seats in the Abbey with friends and family, the importance of the event meant that every ruling house on the continent was asked to send its representatives. In the end, regal attendees included King Harald and Queen Sonja of Norway, Queen Margrethe of Denmark and then-Queen Sofia of Spain as well as the Grand Duke and Duchess of Luxembourg and a host of heirs to thrones. There was also significant representation from the Commonwealth and politicians, as well as places for people from many of the charities that William had been involved with throughout his royal life.

The night before the wedding, many of the royal guests enjoyed a gala evening at a central London hotel with the Queen and members of the royal family joining the celebrations. However, the bride and groom weren't there. William spent his last night as a single man at his father's London home, Clarence House. He was rumoured to have only got about half an hour's sleep due to his nervousness and the screaming fans outside the property when he emerged in the fading light for an impromptu walkabout, where he confessed his nerves to wellwishers. Kate, meanwhile, was staying at the Goring Hotel in London. She arrived with her family, waving nervously as her mum, Carole, and sister Pippa looked on. The following morning, Kate began her

RIGHT Kate's younger sister, Pippa, was the maid of honour, seen here wrangling the bridesmaids

BELOW The Queen chose to wear bright primrose yellow for the wedding so that she could be easily seen by the huge crowds

"Kate began her preparations as a royal bride, keeping her dress a secret until the last minute"

preparations as a royal bride, keeping her dress a secret until the last minute by emerging under heavy screening.

On 29 April 2011, millions tuned in to watch William and Kate finally tie the knot. Despite his lack of sleep, William arrived fresh-faced and smiling at Westminster Abbey in the red uniform of the Irish Guards, the unit of which he was a colonel. Accompanied by Prince Harry, his best man, he was followed by the Middleton family and the royal family, with the Queen and Prince Philip being the last to arrive before the bridal party.

The designer who had won the biggest commission of the 21st century was kept under wraps until the morning of the wedding. Even if the bookies were so certain of the name, they had stopped taking bets. In the end, they were right. Speculation had mounted in the weeks before the wedding that Sarah Burton at Alexander McQueen would design the dress. To keep utmost secrecy, the entrance of the Goring Hotel, where the Middleton family stayed the night before the wedding, was covered in a marquee so that the bride could slide into the Rolls Royce unobserved at 10.51am on the day. The dress was an instant hit. When she stepped out of the car at the steps of the Abbey, she stunned everyone in her McQueen satin and lace A-line dress. Designed with modern takes on Victorian styling, including a narrow waisted bodice with slightly padded hips, it was covered in lace that carried floral motifs including roses, lillies and shamrocks and was rumoured to have cost £250,000. The gown was made of ivory satin, with the bodice fastened at the back with buttons made from gazar and organza. The full-length skirt was created to echo the petals of an opening flower, with soft pleats for added structure. It fanned out into a long, rounded train, while Kate also wore a short, tulle veil held in place with a piece of royal history. She also had a blue bow sewn into the dress for good luck, just like her late mother-in-law had done when she married Prince Charles in 1981.

Kate would step into the church as a commoner and leave as a royal, so it was widely expected that she would don a tiara for her big day. Her choice was filled with significance. Her veil was held by a Cartier Scroll Tiara, made in 1936 and lent to her by the

BELOW Kate and William's horse-drawn carriage, the 1902 State Landau, was the same carriage that carried Charles and Diana from their wedding 30 years earlier

Queen – almost the final royal seal of approval. The Tiara, a sparkling all-diamond diadem, was made for the Queen Mother while she was still Duchess of York and presented to her by her devoted husband on their wedding anniversary. The significance of England's next queen consort wearing a tiara belonging to the last woman to hold that position was lost on nobody.

Kate complemented her wedding tiara with a pair of earrings given to her by her parents. Carole and Michael Middleton had the diamond drop earrings specially made for their daughter, asking jewellers Robinson Pelham to incorporate acorns and oak leaves in the design to echo their new coat of arms. The bride's only other gems that day would be the simple wedding band made of Welsh gold, which she would wear, honouring a tradition that began with the Queen Mother at her own wedding at Westminster Abbey in 1923.

ABOVE "You look lovely," were the first words William said to his bride as she arrived at the altar with her father, Michael

RIGHT Kate and her father, followed by her bridal party, walk between the oak trees brought into Westminster Abbey as part of the decorations

Even Kate's bouquet was designer, having been created by Shane Connolly. It was a fusion of the Middletons' and the royal family's favourites, with each stem holding a meaning. The dominant flower was lily of the valley, which is seen to be a favourite for summer weddings and symbolises a return to happiness, but there was also some sweet William in there as a tender nod to her groom and to represent gallantry. Also included in the bridal posy were small hyacinths, representing the constancy of love, and ivy, which stands for fidelity. Kate followed royal tradition by carrying some sprigs of traditional myrtle taken from bushes first planted by Queen Victoria at Osborne House on the Isle of Wight, who introduced myrtle as a marital tradition into the royal family. The plant has since featured in the bouquets of so many royal brides as the emblem of marriage.

After arriving at Westminster Abbey, Kate joined her bridal party, led by Pippa, who was dressed in a simple white, fitted dress with a cowl neck, made of satin-based crepe. It turned her into an instant star.

After Pippa had helped make the final adjustments to her sister's wedding dress, she took control of the bridesmaids and pageboys who would follow Kate down the aisle. Lady Louise Windsor, Margarita Armstrong-Jones, Grace van Cutsem and Eliza Lopes were dressed in white gowns with lace details, made by Nicki Macfarlane. The two pageboys, Tom Pettifer and William Lowther-Pinkerton, wore Regency-style military uniforms. They walked in procession behind the bride and her father, then maid of honour Pippa, as the Abbey was filled with the strains of Hubert Parry's 'I Was Glad'.

William was forced to keep looking forwards at this point. But that didn't stop Harry from leaning over and whispering, "She looks stunning". William couldn't contain his excitement at finally seeing his bride,

"Her veil was held by a Cartier Scroll Tiara, made in 1936 and lent to her by the Queen – almost the final royal seal of approval"

telling Kate over and over again that she was beautiful.

The service itself was a magnificent affair. Three high-ranking members of the Church of England clergy had the leading roles. The couple giggled and smiled as the ceremony got underway with the Dean of Westminster, John Hall, presiding before the then Archbishop of Canterbury, Rowan Williams, conducted the marriage. Richard Chartres, then Bishop of London, gave the address. He had played a big role in William's life, having confirmed him into the Church of England and quoted St Catherine of Siena, whose feast day falls on 29 April, telling William and Kate to "be who God meant you to be and you will set the world on fire". Members of Kate's family also had their roles in the ceremony. While Pippa was maid of honour, her brother, James, read the lesson – the only reading – while the congregation sang three hymns – 'Guide Me, O Thou Great Redeemer', 'Jerusalem' and 'Love Divine, All Loves Excelling', which had also been used at the blessing of the marriage of the Prince of Wales and the Duchess of Cornwall in 2005. The service lasted just over an hour and the couple became Their Royal Highnesses, the Duke and Duchess of Cambridge but, more importantly, husband and wife.

As part of the wedding celebrations, the Queen had given Prince William three new titles and so, as Kate left Westminster Abbey, she did so as Her Royal Highness the Duchess of Cambridge, Countess of Strathearn and Lady Carrickfergus. On the way out of the Abbey, they stopped to bow to the Queen and then it was on to the reception at Buckingham Palace. They paraded through London in the 1902 State Landau carriage that was originally built for Edward VII's coronation on a route that took them through Whitehall, which was lined with an honour guard comprising the RAF, the Grenadier Guards, the Scots Guards and other regiments, as well as tens of thousands of people cheering them every step of the way, before arriving the palace.

It was there that the couple disappeared inside before making their way onto the balcony for their now famous appearance that featured the rare second kiss in front of the huge crowd that had gathered. The new Duchess of Cambridge was so shocked by the size of the crowds she was seen to say "wow" as she stepped out for her first experience of a royal tradition. The couple were joined by their family for a flypast, featuring a Spitfire and a Hurricane. Then, to huge cheers, the couple sealed their romance with the kisses, both hiding shy smiles as they puckered up for the tens of millions watching around the world. While the rest of their family pretended not to notice, one bridesmaid, Grace van Cutsem, stole the show as she stood in front of the newlyweds looking very grumpy and with her hands firmly over her ears.

Inside Buckingham Palace, Kate and William greeted all of their guests personally before heading into their wedding breakfast. Hundreds of people joined them for a celebratory meal of marinated salmon, crab and langoustines served on a fresh herb

ABOVE The newlywed Duke and Duchess of Cambridge were cheered by hundreds of thousands of people on their carriage ride through London

> *"The bridegroom couldn't contain his excitement at seeing his bride, telling her that she was beautiful"*

ABOVE Prince Harry brings up the rear as the bridal party leave Westminster Abbey following Kate and William's perfectly executed royal wedding

salad followed by a saddle of lamb with Jersey potatoes and asparagus, which was all rounded off with Berkshire honey ice cream, sherry trifle and chocolate parfait.

The couple later cut their spectacular wedding cake. Created by Fiona Cairns, the traditional fruit cake was made at the beginning of March to allow it as much time as possible to mature before the April wedding. Kate had a big say in the final design of the cake, taking a keen interest in how the 900 sugar-paste flowers representing 17 different blooms would be used as decoration. The floral symbols of the four parts of the United Kingdom were represented on the cake, as were lily of the valley, echoing Kate's wedding bouquet, with roses and orange blossom adding a bridal touch. The final cake was eight tiers and weighed over 99 kilograms (220 pounds).

At 3.30pm, it was time to leave once again and the couple sped off to Clarence House for a change of clothes. William drove Kate the short distance in the blue Aston Martin DB6 Volante that had been given to his dad for his 21st birthday and had been modified a little by Harry with tin cans and a number plate reading 'JU5T WED'. The couple were treated to a surprise appearance by a Sea King helicopter as they set off.

They had just a few hours to themselves before appearing before the press once again as they headed out to their evening party – a private dinner at Buckingham Palace, hosted by Charles, followed by dancing with close friends and family. Kate wore another Sarah Burton gown, this time a pure white, off-the-shoulder ball dress with full skirt and sparkling sash, rounded off with a shrug jacket. Ellie Goulding performed at the event, with her rendition of 'Your Song', chosen as the music for the first dance, and the whole affair finished with a small firework display in the palace grounds at 3am.

Kate was ready for another close-up just hours later when she walked out, hand in hand, with her new husband. She and William smiled broadly as they crossed the lawns at Buckingham Palace to a waiting helicopter, which would whisk them away to their secret honeymoon destination. While they were finally able to relax, every detail of their wedding was enjoyed, pored over and appreciated all over again. After a long modern royal romance that saw their love played out on a global stage, they had begun an entirely new chapter of their lives, kicking it off with the ultimate wedding to remember.

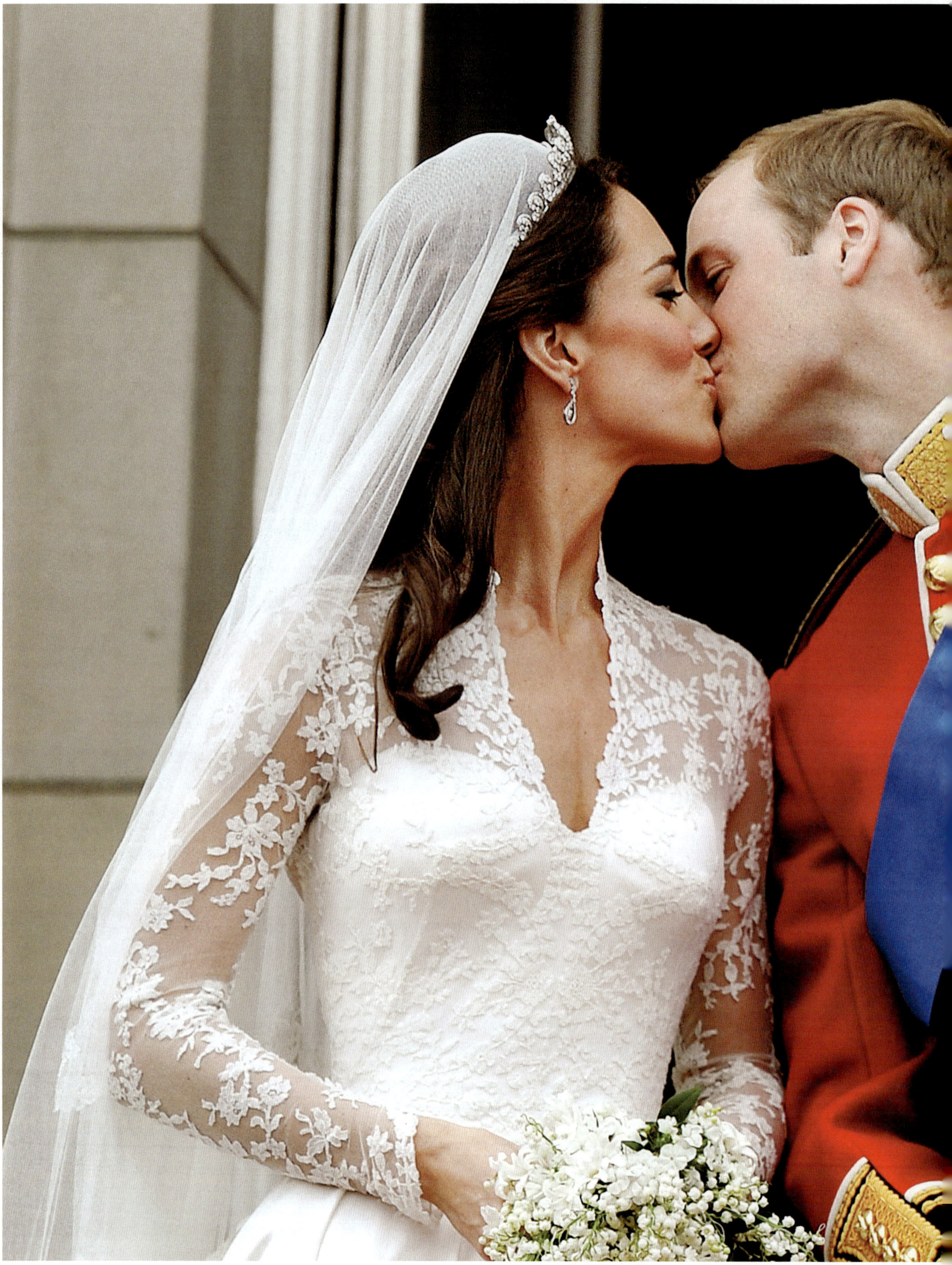

Kate and William during one of their two wedding day kisses on the balcony of Buckingham Palace just after their marriage at Westminster Abbey

The IN-LAWS

Not everybody can boast a king for a father-in-law, but the Prince and Princess of Wales both understand the value of strong family bonds

Across the world, press and public alike just can't get enough of behind-the-scenes gossip from the royal palaces, and stories of family discord and domestic drama command the headlines on a regular basis. Yet, not all family relationships in the House of Windsor and not every story turns into a soap opera. In the case of William and Catherine, a Prince and Princess of Wales who come from very different backgrounds indeed, marriage has forged strong bonds between the couple and their respective families. They are proof that not all in-laws need to be a punchline.

When reports started coming in that Prince William was dating Catherine Middleton, a fellow student at St Andrew's University, the previously unknown young woman found herself catapulted overnight into stardom. It was a shock that was to prove challenging, but with the support and love of their families and friends, they were able to make their relationship a success. Now, after more than a decade of marriage, the Prince and Princess of Wales have become central to the modern monarchy.

In a sometimes turbulent world and one in which leaks to the press – sometimes from the most intimate sources – are an occupational hazard, trust can be all too easily misplaced. In Michael and Carole Middleton, however, the Prince of Wales has been fortunate enough to gain the sort of parents-in-law that seem close to ideal. The prince's entire life has been lived in the spotlight and his own parents' unhappy marriage remains the subject of heated debate, as does his father's relationship with his second wife, Queen Camilla, so keeping his own wife safe from the pressures of life in the royal family was a duty that weighed heavily on him. When the prince met the Middletons, however, he found a couple who were utterly unfazed at having a member of the royal family at the dinner table. The Middletons welcomed the student prince into their family and, crucially, offered a degree of normalcy that some more traditionally arranged royal romances lacked. It was a normalcy that he had craved all his life, and that gave his relationship with his then-girlfriend a strong foundation.

From the early days of their relationship until today, the Prince and Princess of Wales have been at pains to make the point that both sides of their family are equally important, regardless of their royal origins or otherwise. Having lost his mother at a young age, the Prince of Wales relished the opportunity to spend time with a family that had grown up unburdened by duty and protocol, and which had avoided the house of Windsor's widely publicised pitfalls and heartbreaks.

He has spoken with admirable openness and warmth about his love and admiration for the Middletons, particularly their skills as parents and their down-to-earth approach when it comes to raising their children. In fact, William has admitted that he has taken his lead as a father from them, preferring to be a practical and hands-on dad, rather than a formal and unapproachable royal parent.

Whenever the Waleses visit the princess' parents, which they do regularly, the Prince of Wales is just another member of the family. He mucks in around the house, washes the car and enjoys a relaxed relationship with his brother and sister-in-law, James and Pippa. To be treated like any other member of the family was

RIGHT King Charles and Queen his consort, Camilla Parker-Bowles are devoted grandparents to Will and Kate's three children

Image: Getty

something that the prince wanted from the off, as he has revealed in conversations about the early days of the romance. Concerned at how the Middletons' lives would be impacted by their daughter's new boyfriend, the now-Prince of Wales visited her parents at home in order to discuss what the future might hold once things got serious. Having seen his mother's unhappy plight, he was at pains to tell the couple that history wouldn't repeat itself: their daughter would be prepared and protected and so would they. When he gave them his personal phone number and told them to call any time they needed to talk, he put in place the building blocks of the loving relationship that has since developed.

The Prince of Wales, however, didn't ask his future father-in-law for permission to propose, just in case he said no. Happily, the Middletons couldn't have been happier to welcome their new son-in-law and the closeness of their bond was seen around the globe in a touching exchange during the couple's wedding at Westminster Abbey in 2011. As they stood at the altar in the glare of the world's cameras, the Duke of Cambridge leaned across to Michael Middleton as he gave the bride away, and teased, "just a quiet family wedding, then."

Yet, a quiet family life is exactly what the royal couple have done their best to build for their own children. Indeed, despite a nursery filled with nannies and nurses, when the then-Duke and Duchess of Cambridge became parents for the first time, it was to Carole and Michael Middleton

> *"For the Prince of Wales, time spent with the Middletons is pure escapism"*

BELOW Picture here, Carole and Michael Middleton brought their family up in a loving home and provided their three children, Kate, Pippa, and James, with every opportunity they could manage

that they turned. They and the infant Prince George welcomed Carole into their home on Anglesey and, with her help, learned the basics of caring for a newborn not as distant royal parents, but as a hands-on mum and dad.

Given their closeness of their bond, it's no surprise that the princess' parents have joined the royal couple on holidays and at events with other family members, nor that celebrations such as Christmas are split between both sides of the family. For the Prince of Wales, time spent with the Middletons is pure escapism. The most remarkable thing about them for a man raised at the heart of the royal family is that they're so very, entirely normal. It's little wonder that he has spoken warmly of his in-laws, effusively telling the world's press, "I love my in-laws", a statement that leaves no room for debate.

Whilst the Prince of Wales married into a normal family, the challenges facing his wife were considerably more overwhelming. Catherine Middleton, the student he met and fell in love with at university, was to become the Duchess of Cambridge and later Princess of Wales, and she was to be thrust into the world's spotlight, to face the sort of attention that never lets up. In going to visit her parents to explain how their lives would change and to make the gesture of giving them his personal phone number, the prince sent a clear message that their daughter wasn't about to be hung out to dry. Perhaps aware of the situation his mother had found herself in, often feeling isolated and marginalised, he was at pains to avoid a similar situation.

The Princess of Wales, meanwhile, was faced with the challenge of finding a way to fit into a family that is totally unlike any other. She has, of course, been able to do so on a personal level that the public will never be able to experience, coming to know the late Queen Elizabeth II, King Charles III and the rest of the Windsors on an intimate basis. Given some of the personalities involved, that's no mean feat, and is a testament to her easy manner and the support she enjoyed not only from her fiancé - later husband - but from her own family too.

Fortunately for the princess, it became clear once she met her future father-in-law, then the Prince of Wales, that they shared a similar sense of humour. She was approachable and, though respectful, far from awestruck. This quality, along with her openness and support for her husband, have seen her welcomed into the very bosom of the royal household. Bright, witty and pleasant, the princess endeared herself to the late Queen too, who was reportedly delighted to see her grandson with a partner who so obviously made him very happy. By choosing his own wife, rather than having one chosen for him, the Prince of Wales was able to forge a new path for royal marriages.

In a father-son relationship that hasn't always been the best around, the Princess of Wales has managed to find a role for herself as an excellent mediator between the prince and the king, whenever one is required. She has been credited with keeping things on an even keel during periods of tension between the two men, able to see both sides of their tangled and complicated affection, and serving as the cheerful, non-judgemental bridge that could effortlessly connect two, sometimes

BELOW William and Kate with William's grandmother, the late Queen

clashing, personalities. As the years have passed she has grown increasingly close to Charles, and has been at his side when he needed support. When she kissed the then-Prince's cheek after the funeral of his late father, it sent a clear message that this was a royal family who were closer than ever.

The sometimes formidable behaviour of the king seems to have been punctured by his daughter-in-law, who is far more likely to greet him with a cheery "hello, grandfather" or a peck on the cheek than with stiff formality. Just as the Prince of Wales has relished the normality of the Middleton household, his wife has brought that same breath of fresh air to the sometimes stifling royal palaces.

Yet, within those palaces, there are tensions just as in any other family, and as the prince found his relationship with his stepmother, Camilla, scrutinised, royal watchers were keen to see how the princess would relate to her too. Of course, the Princess of Wales has an understanding of the intricacies of the royal family that isn't given to outsiders, and enjoys an insight into husband's feelings regarding his stepmother that certainly won't ever be shared with the public. Though those emotions will remain private, one need only see the Princess of Wales and the Queen Consort together to recognise the friendship that exists between them.

Just like the Princess of Wales, Queen Camilla didn't come from royal stock, so the Queen Consort understands a thing or two about having to fit into the sometimes bewildering royal world. Perhaps that has helped her build a relationship with her stepdaughter-in-law, which will certainly have been strengthened by the clear affection between the king and the princess. They have both observed and been pulled into tumultuous events thanks to their marriages, which can only have helped them to gain an understanding of and respect for one another.

Just as the Prince of Wales forged

ABOVE The Windsors and the Middletons have proven to be a supportive extended family

friendly ties with his siblings-in-law, even before she was engaged, the princess developed a friendly bond with Prince Harry. He later fondly remarked that he looked on her as a sister rather than an in-law and joked that he loved nothing more than to make her laugh. The two bonded when she taught him how to cook and, far from Harry's worries that she would take his brother away, they became a close-knit trio both in public and behind the scenes. Rumour has it that the trio has been fractured in more recent years, but there's no denying that the princess and her brother-in-law, now the Duke of Sussex, were once as close as any siblings.

When the couple married, the late queen awarded William and Catherine the titles Duke and Duchess of Cambridge. They retained those titles until the queen's death and Charles' succession to the throne, at which point they succeeded as Prince and Princess of Wales. As Duke and Duchess of Cambridge, however, the couple deepened their already strong familial bonds when they became parents, making Charles a grandfather for the

the royal couple have been at pains to give their children as normal a childhood as is possible given their circumstances, a world away from the emotional frigidity that seems to have been King Charles' childhood lot.

Unassuming, gracious and open, the Princess of Wales brought a freshness to the royal family upon her marriage that charmed the late queen. Since the death of Diana, Princess of Wales, the monarch had been steadfastly at her grandsons' sides, guiding them through life as well as she could and helping them to navigate some difficult years. In Carole Middleton, William gained a mother figure that came without any baggage or history, and in Catherine, the queen was able to see that he had gained a loving companion too. As the late queen grew older, she often turned to her granddaughter-in-law for support and delegated tours and patronages to her when she was Duchess of Cambridge. Now, as Princess of Wales, she will provide the same support to her father and stepmother-in-law as the monarchy moves into a new era.

Being born into or marrying into the royal family brings with it immense privilege and wealth, but that is counterbalanced with a lack of privacy and intense scrutiny. The Prince and Princess of Wales, however, have forged the strongest bonds imaginable both in their own family and with their respective in-laws.

With the death of the late Queen Elizabeth II, the Prince of Wales has become the heir to the throne and his wife will be his queen. Their loving and affectionate extended family will give them the perfect foundations and support network for this weighty responsibility, offering a refreshing and relatable air of normality that has proven to be popular with the public and royals alike. Though down-to-earth might not be something we associate with the Windsors, the Prince and Prince of Wales are doing their best to change that, and bring the British monarchy into a new era.

> **WC** *"The couple deepened their already strong familial bonds when they became parents"*

first time. Though he has often suffered from a reputation as a man who keeps his emotions tamped down, Charles has been effusive when discussing his grandchildren and enjoys a very strong relationship with the Wales' children. Just as the Middletons enjoy plenty of private time with the grandchildren, so too do Charles and Camilla, who relish entertaining the youngsters away from the prying glare of the media. Once again, the Wales' approach to parenting has brought a welcome degree of informality to the royal household that it has previously seemed to lack. Following the Middletons' example,

Images: Alamy

Keeping up with the CAMBRIDGES

With William and Kate happily married, it was time for them to start building their family and future of the Windsors – and the world didn't have to wait too long for it to happen

When the then Duchess of Cambridge emerged onto the steps of a London hospital looking pale and tired, she had an audience of millions around the world watching her. In early December 2012, Kate faced the cameras for the first time since the news everyone had been waiting for had been confirmed. Although she was ill and in need of rest, she and William were also ready to celebrate. After all, it had just been announced that they were expecting their first baby.

Kate's tummy had become an object of global fascination in the months after her marriage in April 2011, as expectations about a royal pregnancy began to grow. Every move that the new Duchess made was examined for possible clues about an impending royal baby. When Kate declined peanut butter on a visit to Denmark in November 2011, it was seen as a sign that she was expecting, as was her decision to raise a toast using only water while on her Diamond Jubilee Tour in September 2012. In the end, the announcement that the Cambridge family was under way came as a bit of a surprise and was actually forced on William and Kate by the severe morning sickness that the mother-to-be quickly experienced.

The Duchess was so sick with hyperemesis gravidarum in the early weeks of her first trimester that she was admitted to King Edward VII Hospital in London for treatment to make sure that she and her baby were getting enough water and nutrients. As soon as she entered the hospital doors, a pregnancy announcement had to be made. As his wife rested soon after admission, William had spoken to the press, while members of the royal family, including the Queen and William's father, expressed their delight at the news of a new heir to the throne.

Not long after Kate was forced to announce her pregnancy early (royal mothers usually wait until around the 12-week

RIGHT Catherine and William with their children, Prince George, Prince Louis and Princess Charlotte in June 2023 – longer the Duke and Duchess of Cambridge, the couple are now the Prince and Princess of Wales

mark before they publicly share their news), final consent came through from all the Commonwealth countries for a change to the centuries-old law governing the passage of the throne. On 14 January 2013, St James's Palace announced that the baby was to be born in July, and in the months leading up to the birth, the Succession to the Crown Act was hurriedly pushed through parliament, eliminating the gender bias from the line of succession. The act was finally given royal assent in April 2013 and meant that Kate's baby would be guaranteed to succeed as monarch, regardless of their gender because a baby girl could no longer be bumped down the line by a brother born after her. Many celebrated this change, which was being described in the papers as a move to bring the royal family into the 21st century.

But that's not all. As she emerged from the difficult start to her pregnancy, another ground-breaking royal announcement was made. On 31 December 2012, the Queen issued Letters Patent, which decreed that all the children of the eldest son of the then Prince of Wales would be given the title of His or Her Royal Highness and be known as prince or princess. Before this announcement, an HRH was reserved purely for a first-born son. Kate, the first commoner to marry

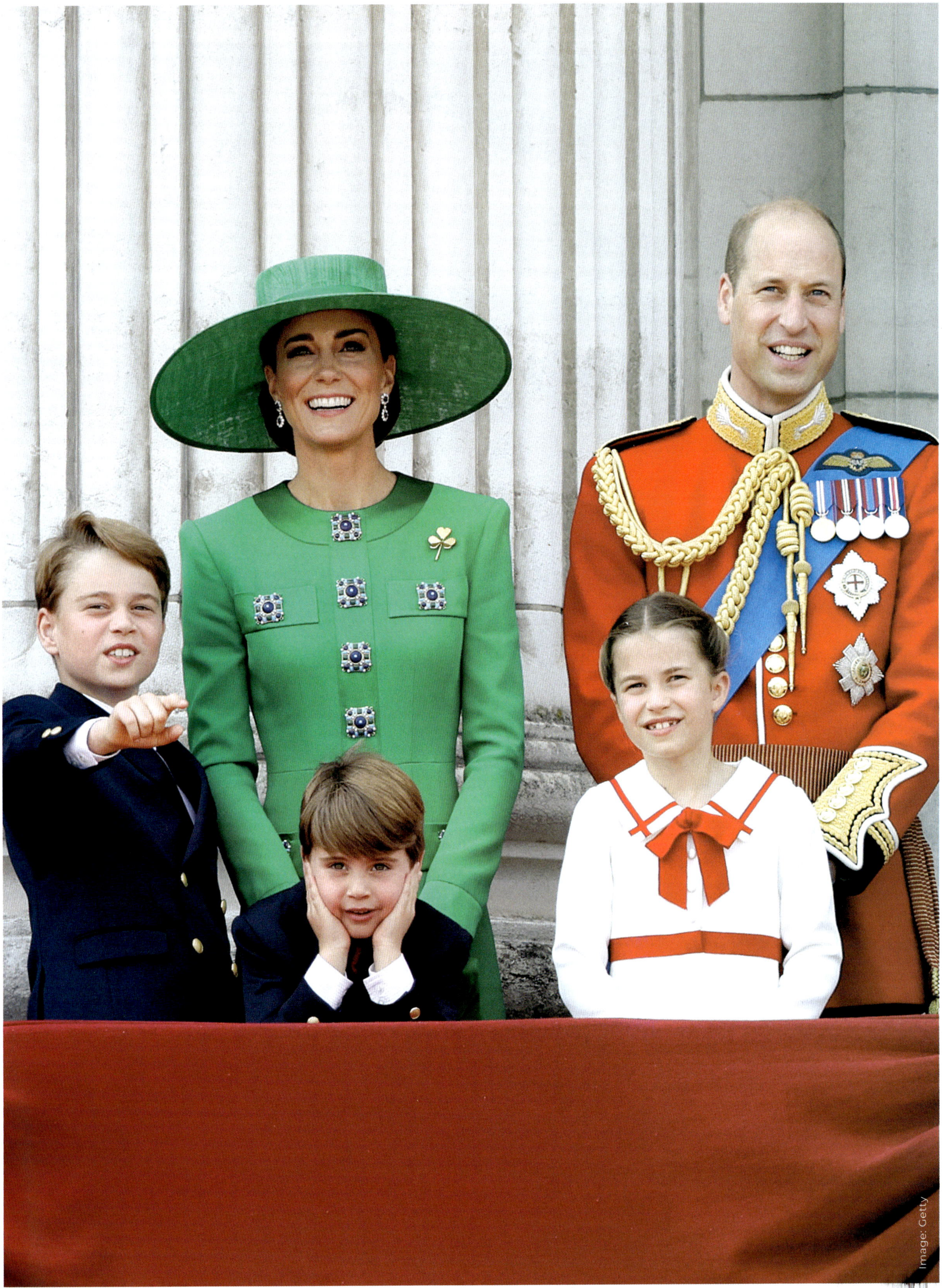

Image: Getty

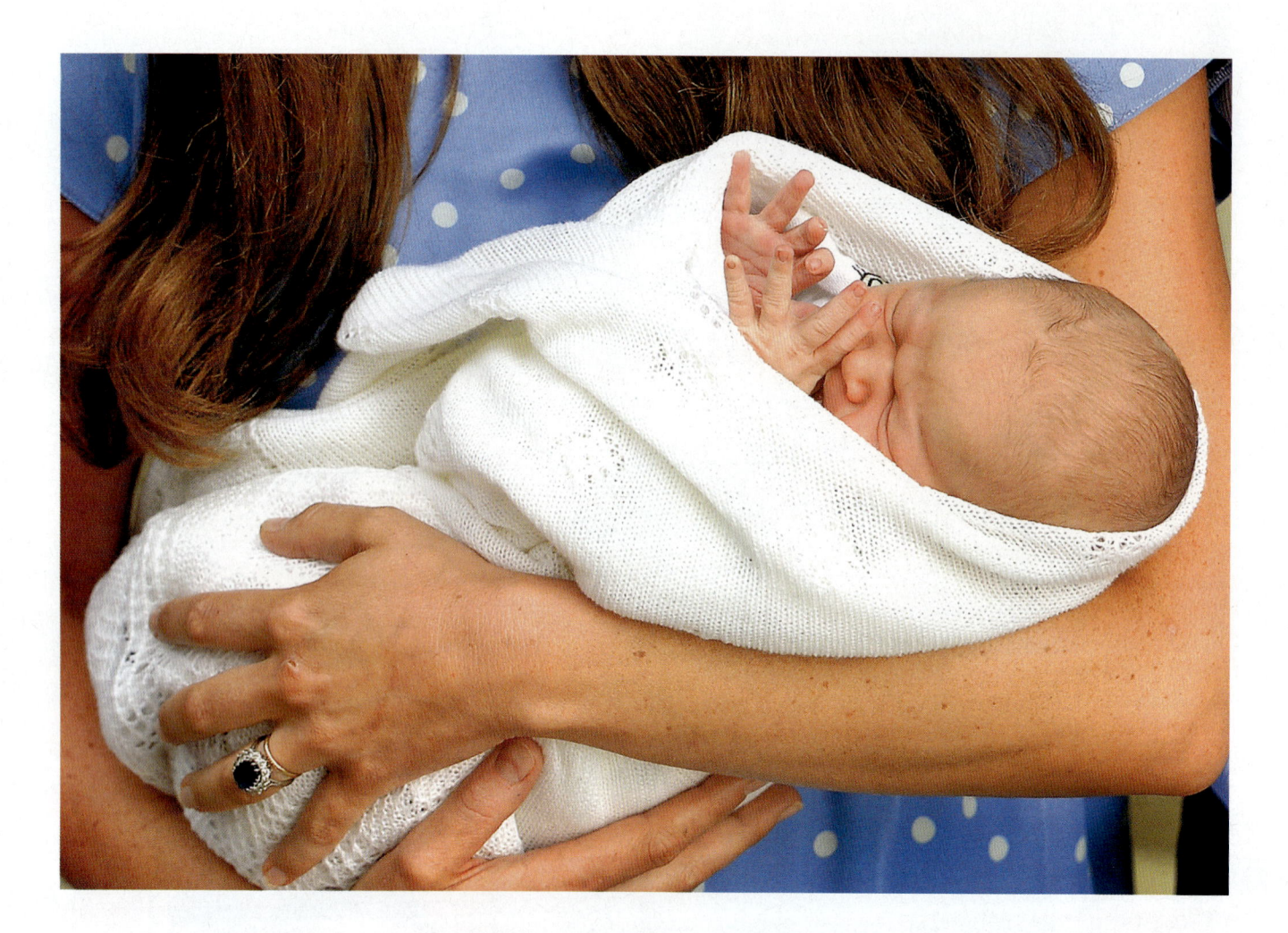

ABOVE Millions of people around the world watch Kate carry her first child, and future king, out of the Lindo Wing at St Mary's Hospital, Paddington, the day after his birth in July 2013

a direct heir to the throne, would now see all her children take royal titles from birth.

Her pregnancy was a very modern one for the royals in other ways, too. From the moment she started carrying out engagements again in January 2013, hundreds of images winged their way around the world as people desperately looked for the first hint of a baby bump. In an age increasingly dominated by social media, there was endless speculation as to the gender of her baby and the name that the Kate and William would pick. In the end the couple decided to go the traditional route. They refused to give any real hint of a precise due date, while – despite on one occasion appearing to stop herself asking whether a present she had been given was for a daughter – Kate also said that she and William didn't know whether they were having a boy or a girl.

In a modern media age, the royal couple were also able to keep the actual birth of their baby to themselves for several hours despite the hospital where they welcomed their child being surrounded by press. On 22 July 2013, Kensington Palace confirmed that the Duchess of Cambridge had been admitted to the Lindo Wing of St Mary's Hospital, Paddington, just after 6am in the early stages of labour. Around 8pm that day, it was announced that Kate had given birth to a healthy baby boy. The first time William had been to the Lindo Wing since the birth of his brother, he was by his wife's side when Kate gave birth to their first child, a 8lbs 6oz son, earlier that day at 4.24pm and spent time enjoying life as a family before sharing their news with the world. The baby was delivered by the Queen's surgeon-gynaecologist, Sir Marcus Setchell, while a team of 20 other experts were on standby just in case of any emergency.

For decades, royal births had been announced with an official, typewritten communication placed on the railings of Buckingham Palace. When Kate's baby arrived, that note was instead shown on an easel to make it easier to see, and the first details of the royal birth had been sent out in a press release, emailed to reporters around the world. Meanwhile, an unofficial town crier took to the steps of the Lindo Wing to announce the birth of a future king.

Some traditions remained untouched. After the royal baby was born, 21-gun salutes were fired in London, across the UK and in Commonwealth countries including Canada and New Zealand. The bells of Westminster Abbey also rang out to welcome the child. The day after his birth, the baby was visited by the Prince of Wales and Kate's parents.

Just over 24 hours after delivering her first baby, Kate stepped out to present him to the world. The Duke and Duchess of Cambridge emerged from the Lindo Wing in the late afternoon of 23 July to greet the wall of paparazzi, with Kate wearing a blue dress covered in white spots, reminiscent of the outfit Diana had chosen to bring William home from hospital and a clear nod to the mother-

ABOVE George visits the Sensational Butterflies exhibition at the Natural History Museum for his first birthday

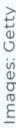

in-law she never knew. The couple were clearly overcome at the rapturous reception they received at the hospital, with both speaking briefly to the press while their son slept through his first photocall. After pausing briefly for photographs on the step, William showed how he and Kate were ready to change some traditions as he delicately placed his newborn son into a car, famously wiping his brow in mock relief after successfully fitting the car seat containing his baby boy into the family's vehicle, before driving his new family to Kensington Palace to begin their life as a family of three.

The following day the baby's name was officially announced. Much to the bookies' relief, the Duke and Duchess of Cambridge picked one of their favourite names for their newborn son. On 24 July 2013, they confirmed they had called their little boy George Alexander Louis, formally known as Prince George of Cambridge. Those were the names the Archbishop of Canterbury pronounced over the Silver Lily Font at St James's Palace, London at the intimate family christening, which took place on 23 October 2013. In keeping with royal tradition, George wore a handmade replica of the royal family's 19th century Honiton lace christening gown, and water from the River Jordan was used. The young Prince posed for official photos, among them an historic image in which he appeared next to his father, grandfather and great-grandmother. It was the first time that a ruling monarch had been able to present three generations of heirs since the reign of Queen Victoria.

Kate and William were determined from the very beginning of their son's life to allow him to grow up away from the public gaze. However, there was a huge appetite for news of George and the little Prince was snapped arriving with his mum for a family holiday when he was just a few months old. His next official appearance came in April 2014 when, just like his father before him, he accompanied his parents on a tour of Australia and New Zealand aged just nine months. This was one of the biggest journeys that the Cambridges had ever undertaken but all eyes were firmly focussed on their little boy. From the moment he crawled onto a rug at a playdate organised for him in Wellington, New Zealand, to the scene-stealing appearance at Taronga Zoo in Sydney, where he almost made it into the pen of a bilby named in his honour, the tour was as much about George as it was his mum and dad. It was clear to everyone how much William loved his son. It was also revealed that William played a hands-on role, regularly feeding him bottles and putting him to bed, although Kate later admitted that William, like many new parents, had initially struggled as he adjusted to his new role as a parent.

By the time official photos were released to mark his first birthday in July 2014, speculation was growing that Kate and William were about to add to their family. Confirmation that a second baby was on the way came in September 2014, when Kate once again found herself experiencing extreme

113

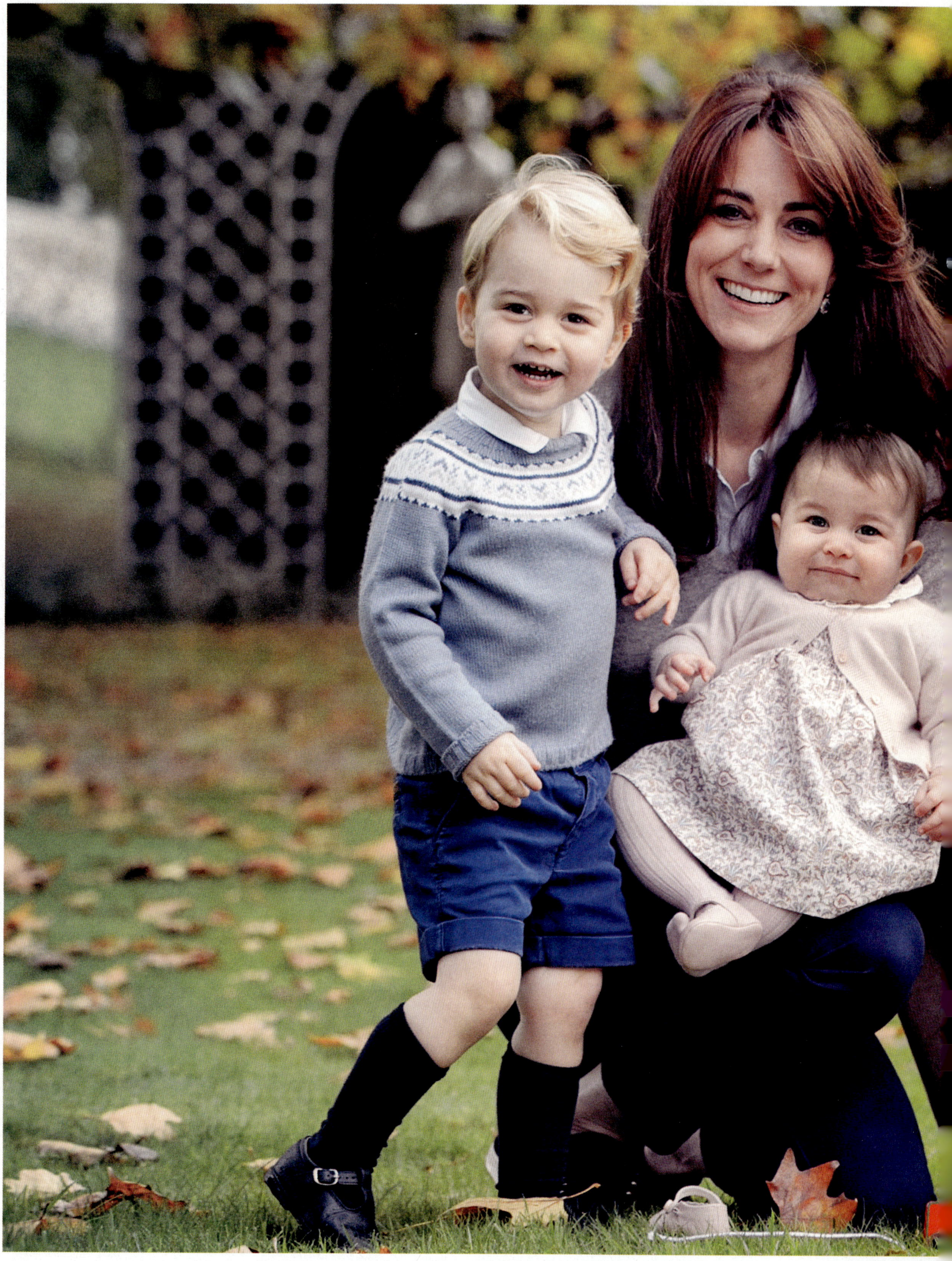

The relaxed family shots, often taken by Kate herself, have become a hallmark of the loving couple.

> *"Speculation was growing that the Cambridges were about to add to their family"*

sickness. Forced to retire from her first overseas solo visit to Malta and from a string of engagements, the Duchess of Cambridge rested at home with her son while royal baby fever whipped up the world once again.

On 8 September 2014, the news was officially announced that there was going to be another addition to the nation's favourite family of three. While the announcement was again made early on in Kate's pregnancy due to her terrible morning sickness, there was nothing but unbridled joy and smiles all round.

Kate's first official appearance after her second pregnancy was confirmed came at the start of the State Visit of the President of Singapore, when the Duchess accompanied her husband at a welcome ceremony for the royal guests and confided that she was pleased to be able to get out of the house again. There was just as much excitement over Kate's great expectations the second time around and, as with her pregnancy with George, her choice of maternity clothes became fashion must-haves. Speculation that the little Prince would get a baby sister went into overdrive when Kate wore a bright pink coat on her final public appearance before maternity leave but, just as before, the royal couple had no idea of the gender of their second child ahead of the birth.

Kate was admitted to the Lindo Wing in the early hours of Saturday 2 May 2015, after going into labour that morning. As with the birth of Prince George, royal doctors Guy Thorpe-Beeston and Alan Farthing were on hand to care for Kate as she brought her second child into the world. Her daughter was delivered at 8.34am that morning. News of her birth was shared just after 11am and showing the difference just a few years can make, the announcement was placed on social media as well as in emailed press releases, while Kensington Palace set up its own Instagram account around the same time to be able to share news of the growing Cambridge family. Kate left hospital with her little girl just hours later, but not before Prince George had walked shyly into St Mary's to see his mum and brand-new little sister.

Later that afternoon, the Duke and Duchess of Cambridge appeared on the steps of St Mary's Hospital with the new princess in Kate's arms. The second-time mum chose bright yellow for this appearance, wearing a floral printed dress by Jenny Packham, while her daughter was warmly wrapped up

BELOW Kate has already taken George and Charlotte on several tours, including her 2016 visit to Canada, where they joined in the fun at a party in honour of military families

against the spring breezes in a woollen cap, which had been bought by the family of the Cambridge's nanny, Maria Borrallo.

Two days later, her name was announced: Charlotte Elizabeth Diana, the second and third names from her great-grandmother the Queen and William's mother respectively. The family soon retreated to their country home, Anmer Hall in Norfolk, where Kate took the first official photos of the princess as she snuggled in the arms of her big brother.

To mark the birth, landmarks such as Tower Bridge, the London Eye and the Peace Tower in Canada, were lit up pink, and gun salutes were fired at Hyde Park and the Tower of London.

Kate and William again tried to shield their family from media interest, but they were surrounded by the world's press – as well as big crowds – for Charlotte's christening, which took place on 5 July 2015 on the Sandringham Estate in Norfolk, also with water from the River Jordan and the handmade christening robe replica. In another nod to royal tradition, she was taken from the royal estate to St Mary Magdalene Church for the ceremony, again conducted by the Archbishop of Canterbury, nestled in a vintage Millson pram just like both her uncles Prince Andrew and Prince Edward had been. It was also a poignant link to the grandmother whose name she shared – William's mother, Diana, had been christened in the same church in 1961. Members of the local community were also invited to join in with the happy occasion outside the church.

Princess Charlotte's first official public appearance – after appearing with her parents outside of the Lindo Wing on the day after her birth, that is – was on the balcony of Buckingham Palace on 11 June 2016. As well as marvelling at how adorable the two youngest members of the Cambridge family were, the world was also treated to a glimpse of what William's role as a father was. As Charlotte was being held by her mother while they watched the flypast with the rest of the royal family, William lovingly swept a lock of his daughter's hair behind her ear. He later joked with his son, the two of them chuckling away, with William taking obvious delight at George's unmissable grin as the planes noisily flew overhead.

Charlotte, like her brother, was soon taking on royal tours. She travelled with her parents and George to Canada in September 2014, where she stole the show at a children's party organised for military families. By the time she travelled to Germany and Poland in July 2017, again with brother George in tow, she was a confident two-year-old who even staged a royal sit in on the tarmac of an airport when she decided she had had enough of royal duties.

Sources close to William and Kate have also shared what the family gets up to behind the scenes. While Kate and William are very hands-on, the children also have a Spanish nanny, the aforementioned Maria Teresa Turrion Borrallo, who takes them to the park – possibly William's influence to get his children outside and away from screens, which are seen as toys for the adults, as much as possible – as well as teaching them Spanish words. Another sign that the heirs to the throne are enjoying a relatively normal life is that Maria Teresa bakes and cooks with them. Apparently George loves stealing some of the icing, and both he and Charlotte love making a mess, just like any child let loose in a kitchen.

The year of 2017 was one of change for the family. In September, Prince George had been attending nursery in Norfolk where he'd become a pupil at West Acre Montessori School in January 2016, but his parents decided his primary education should take place in London. Kate and William enrolled their son at Thomas's School

ABOVE As the Cambridges arrived in Germany in July 2017, they showed themselves to be a tight unit

"Kate and William were determined from the very beginning of their son's life to allow him to grow up away from the public gaze"

in Battersea with every expectation that Charlotte would eventually follow him there. Meanwhile, their daughter was lined up to attend The Willcocks Nursery School near to Kensington Palace. With their two children nice and settled, the William and Kate decided to expand their family again. Kate's third pregnancy was announced on 4 September 2017, just months after she'd joked publicly with William that they should have another baby. Again suffering from hyperemesis gravidarum, Kate was forced to miss George's first day at school, but as soon as she was well enough she became a regular on the school run. George was instead taken by his father on his first day of new school, where the relationship between them was obvious as George tried to hide behind his father's legs.

Sources close to the royal family have said that Charlotte struggled with George's absence at first, but that she eventually came round to having her parents and nanny to herself during the day. The family also shared that they had fallen into a comfortable morning rhythm, with boiled eggs and Marmite on toast for breakfast at 6am. Apparently George often proclaimed: "I'm the king of the castle!" to which Charlotte, eager to join in, usually replied: "So am I!"

It was in November 2017 that William once again showed the world his caring side as a father. On a tour of Finland, he personally delivered Prince George's Christmas list to Santa himself, and the four-year-old wanted only one thing: a toy police car. Apparently on Christmas Day, George received the only toy he was after, and was over the moon. William later divulged that George had played a sheep in his school nativity and his father's influence couldn't be more pronounced, as teachers have described the young Prince as sharing his father's passion for sports as well as his competitive streak.

There was another exciting year ahead for the Cambridges, when

Images: Getty

ABOVE Prince Louis Arthur Charles is carried out of the Lindo Wing in his father's arms on 23 April 2018, just six hours after his birth

LEFT The christening of Prince Louis took place on 9 July 2018 at the Chapel Royal, St James's Palace. His siblings looked very smart for the occasion, as they walked alongside their parents

> "Kate has made no secret of her desire for a big family, it may be that Louis isn't the last child"

2018 saw the arrival of William and Kate's third child. On 23 April, a son was safely delivered at 11.01am, with George and Charlotte arriving to meet their little brother for the first time as soon as school was over. Just six hours after his birth, the new fifth-in-line to the throne was taken home. While the announcement was made that a prince had been born, the public was left waiting for a name. Finally, a few days later, on 27 April, the name was revealed as Prince Louis Arthur Charles of Cambridge. The little Prince spent his earliest weeks at Kensington Palace, where he was photographed by his mother just days after his birth, and his christening also took place in London. Louis was baptised on 9 July 2018 at St James's Palace with his new aunt, the Duchess of Sussex, present, but without his great-grandparents, the Queen and the Duke of Edinburgh, who decided not to attend this ceremony.

Louis' earliest years were spent in London as his parents continued to take on an increasing amount of royal engagements and George and Charlotte continued their education. Kate has made no secret of her desire for a big family, and it may well be that Louis isn't the last of her children. However, for now, he has the privilege of being the youngest child of the happy and increasingly popular young family. Anyone will tell you that raising two children, let alone three, is a monumental task, but William and Kate are handling it with poise and grace as they bring up the next generation of royals.

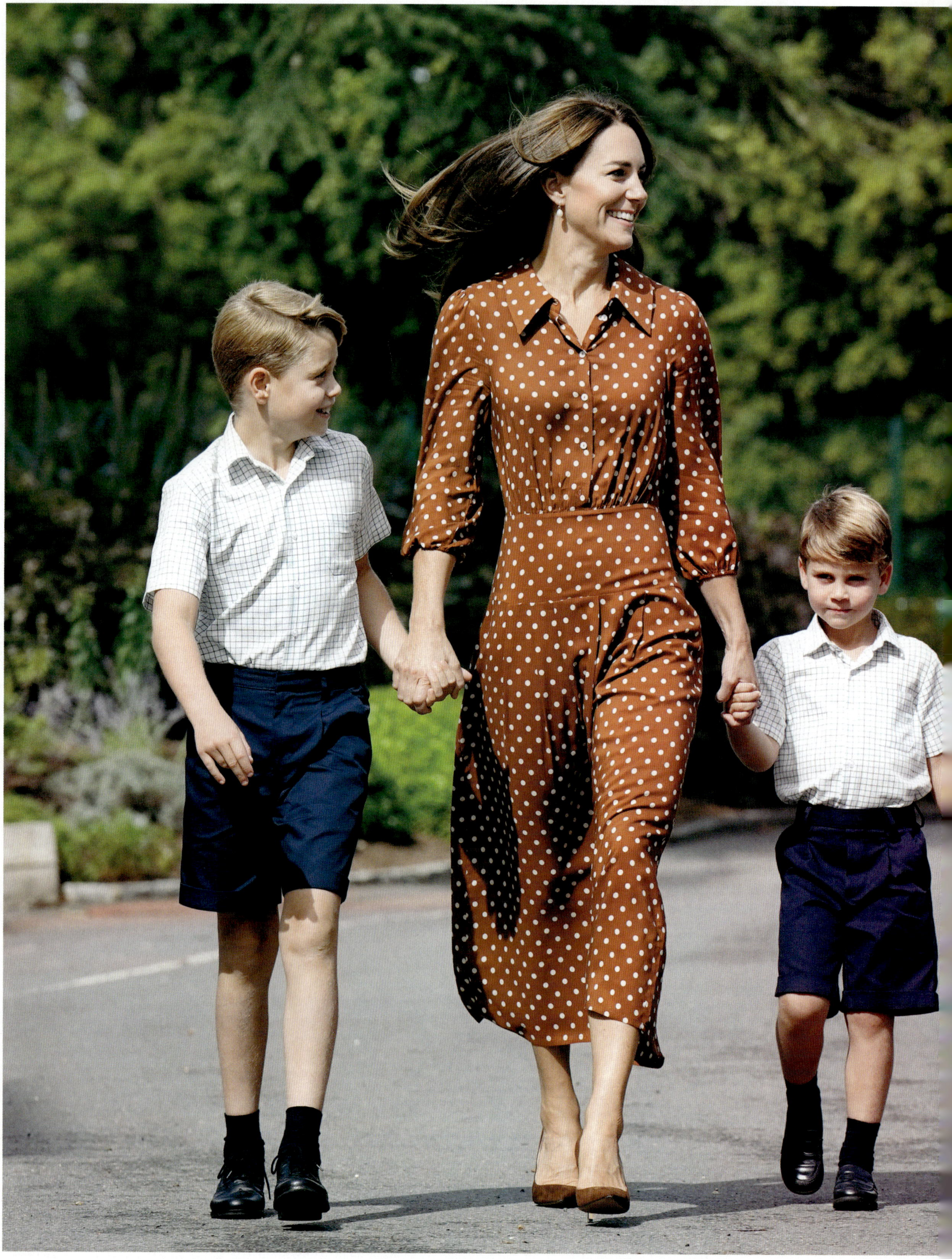

WC

William and Catherine are determined to bring up their children in the most 'normal' way possible for members of royalty

MODERNISING the MONARCHY

In a changing world, the House of Windsor is looking to the future. Central to its vision are the Prince and Princess of Wales

On 8 September 2022, Queen Elizabeth II died at Balmoral, having reigned as monarch of the United Kingdom for 70 years. She was the longest serving British monarch and her son, Charles, Prince of Wales, had been waiting to succeed to the throne for almost as long as his mother had occupied it. His succession as King Charles III signalled a new phase in the British monarchy and he has promised reforms intended to tackle both the management and scope of the royal households, as well as questions regarding the institution itself.

The world today is a very different place to the world in which the late queen came to the throne, and the new king and his heirs are all too aware of the importance of modernisation and changing with the sometimes tumultuous times. It is a time of unprecedented change for the monarchy, but it is a time that King Charles has been preparing for for a whole lifetime. It is testament to his awareness of his role and duty that he has been preparing his heir apparent, the Prince of Wales, too.

The death of the late queen saw a raft of changes immediately take place, some more obvious than others. At the moment of her passing Charles, as her eldest son and heir, immediately succeed her as sovereign. Behind the scenes many other things began to change too, from stamps to coins to post boxes, and for some members of the royal family, it was all change when it came to titles too. However, one of the most famous titles of all was vacated, as the Prince of Wales succeeded to the crown and left his old title behind.

Though the heir to the throne assuming the title of Prince of Wales is an age-old tradition that can be traced back through the centuries, many people were surprised to learn that there was no automatic right of succession to the title

RIGHT The Prince and Princess of Wales are pictured on the balcony of Buckingham Palace with their son, Prince George, on after King Charles III's coronation

for the new king's oldest son, and nor is it guaranteed to be awarded to the eldest son and heir. Instead, Prince William did become heir apparent, and he and Catherine automatically received a slew of new titles including those of Duke and Duchess of Cornwall, which had previously been held by Charles and the new queen consort, Camilla. The title of Prince of Wales, however, is one that is given at the discretion of the sovereign, so it remained vacant in the hours immediately following the death of the queen and the succession of the king.

That vacancy was filled when King Charles made his first speech as monarch on 9 September 2022, just 24 hours after the late queen died. Speaking from the Blue Drawing Room at Buckingham Palace on the day after the death of his mother, a sorrowful and emotional Charles officially bestowed the title of Prince of Wales on his son, William, in a move that had been widely anticipated by royal-watchers across the world. In the same speech, he bestowed the title of Princess of Wales on William's wife, Catherine, making her the first person to use that style since the death of the late Diana, Princess of Wales. Though Charles had married his second wife,

Image: Getty

Camilla, in 2005, and she immediately became Princess of Wales upon the occasion of their marriage, she chose to be styled instead as Duchess of Cornwall. Though she has never spoken publicly about this decision, it is believed that Camilla wished to use a different title out of respect to the memory of Diana and her sons, to whom Camilla was now stepmother.

Until the official notification of the title change given in the king's speech, William and Catherine had retained the titles of Duke and Duchess of Cambridge, which had been given to them on their wedding day by the late queen. The king also used his speech to pay heartfelt tribute to both of his sons and their wives and families, but with the Duke and Duchess of Sussex stepping back from royal duties, it was with the Prince and Princess of Wales that responsibility for the future was seen to rest. "With Catherine beside him," the king said during his address to the nation, "Our new Prince and Princess of Wales will, I know, continue to inspire and lead our national conversations". It was an indication that Charles was determined to see continuity, when the press and public were busy looking for signs of upheaval at the heart of the changing royal family.

When Queen Elizabeth II died after her record-breaking and era-defining reign, she had proved herself as a monarch again and again, gaining the respect of people not just at home, but all over the globe. By now in his 74th year, her son and successor has considerably less years ahead of him in which to make an impact, but he is determined to do so. He has spoken often about his plans to slim down the monarchy and make it an efficient institution properly suited to and reflective of the 21st century. As central, senior members of the House of Windsor, the Prince and Princess of Wales are key to his vision, and inside sources claim that he is very aware of the importance of Catherine's popularity in particular. Indeed, some have termed her the monarchy's secret weapon as it looks to the future.

Though public polls during the last years of the late queen's lifetime suggested that the majority of respondents hoped that he would abdicate his responsibilities and allow Prince William to succeed his grandmother, there was never any realistic proposition that this would happen. Just as King Charles has spent a lifetime preparing for his role, he has taken a lesson in service from his late mother that would simply not allow him to take such a drastic step. Having waited in the wings for 70 years, the king is all too aware of the weight of the burden he has assumed, and so too has he always intended for his heir to be fully prepared before he becomes the sovereign. Busy with their various royal duties and raising a young family, the Prince and Princess of Wales certainly have plenty to occupy their time whilst the king gets on with the business of ruling.

Whether at the funeral of the Duke of Edinburgh or the late queen, the Prince and Princess of Wales have been rocks at the side of Charles. When the new king was corned at Westminster Abbey on 6 May 2023, they made headlines by arriving late, but other than that small blot on their copybook, the family undertook their duty with aplomb. Whilst the princess had no formal part in the ceremony, she took her place on the front row alongside her husband and children. For the prince, meanwhile, there was a moment in the spotlight when he swore allegiance to his father.

BELOW The couple and their son, Prince George, are pictured during Queen Elizabeth II's funeral

> *"Our new Prince and Princess of Wales will continue to inspire and lead our national conversations"*

During this solemn moment, the king sat on the throne as the Archbishop of Canterbury and Prince of Wales offered him their oath of fealty. After a kneeling William had pledged his loyalty and "liege man of life and limb", he placed his hand on the crown his father was wearing, then kissed his cheek. A clearly emotional King Charles murmured, "thank you, William", in an exchange picked up by the world's cameras.

In the midst of the grandeur of the coronation, this unscripted moment between a father and son who have famously not always seen eye to eye touched viewers with its simplicity. When the key members of the royal family appeared on the balcony to greet crowds who had gathered on the Mall after the ceremony, the Prince and Princess of Wales were central to the very select group afforded that honour. Likewise, when Charles undertook a walkabout on 5 May, the eve of his coronation, it was William and Catherine who accompanied him. This show of solidarity and good-natured affection sent a clear message about in whose hands the future of the monarchy was held.

The warmth between the two men was further highlighted when the Prince of Wales gave a heartfelt and celebratory speech in honour of his father at the Coronation Concert the following day. As crowds gathered to watch the show, William took to the stage to pay tribute to his late grandmother and tell Charles, "pa, we are all so proud of you". It was a sentiment that the king would no doubt have echoed as he watched his son and heir address the crowd, as well as television viewers across the world. Though there has been much debate about the new king's decision to slim down the monarchy to a key group of senior working royals, there can be

BELOW William and Kate are pictured ordering and delivering pizza during their tour of Wales

no doubt that his son and daughter-in-law are at the heart of his plans to modernise the institution that he is now in charge of.

The Wales' path to the throne is one that was mapped out long ago, and the prince had a sense of duty instilled in him from childhood. When he married Catherine, she enthusiastically took her place on the royal merry-go-round of tours and visits, charities and patronages. Those responsibilities increased when the elderly queen began to scale back her official duties in her later years, both in order to spend more time resting and so that her son and grandson could get a taste of what life would be like when she was gone. Now Charles has succeeded as king and William has succeeded as Prince of Wales, both will find that their lives have changed.

Now King Charles is reigning, more of his time than ever before will be taken up with matters of state, meaning that he has already had to make some difficult decisions regarding his external interests and patronages. As he has had to focus more on his monarchical duties, much of the role he fulfilled when he was heir to the throne has passed to William, his own heir. Just as Charles spent many years building his role and responsibilities both to reflect his own interests and prepare for the responsibility that one day awaited him, it is a dual role that William too will have to juggle. On the one hand, the Prince of Wales is the father of three young children and has spoken often and openly about his wish to raise his family to be as normal and down to earth as possible. On the other hand, however, he is a senior working royal and the heir to the throne, with all the duties that entails. It's little wonder that Charles wants him to prepare as much as possible for his own succession by serving as Prince of Wales for as long as that might take. Even as they settle into their new roles, William and Catherine will be thinking about preparing their own

ABOVE George, Charlotte and Louis joined their parents as they volunteered with the 3rd Upton Scouts during the Big Help Out

RIGHT The Princess of Wales puts her archery skills to the test as her husband and eldest son look on

eldest son, George, for his own path to the throne. The line of succession never stops, after all.

Whilst the Prince of Wales focuses on the duties that await him one day and learns the ropes of his new role, his wife will also see some changes to her own position as a working royal. She has thrown herself with enthusiasm and verve into life as a member of the royal family, scoring hit after hit with her public appearances and deft eye for public relations, but her diary will be filling up more quickly than ever now. When they were Duke and Duchess of Cambridge, the royal couple undertook visits to Europe on official engagements and toured India and Bhutan, amongst others, but those overseas visits will likely increase exponentially now. As William's role expands and his father grows older, it's very likely that the couple will be called upon to be representives for the royal family at more and more overseas events.

Likewise, it's highly likely that the new Prince and Princess of Wales will now be called upon to play a bigger than ever role in state visits. The monarch welcomes an average of two overseas heads of state to the UK annually for prestigious special occasions, which are intended to forge and strengthen diplomatic ties. Whilst King Charles will shoulder the responsibility for the central occasions on these events, other working royals are expected to take the lead on other elements of these state visits. As heir to

"There can be no doubt that his son and daughter-in-law are at the heart of his plans to modernise the institution"

the throne, the Prince and Princess of Wales will be expected to play the lead role on such occasions.

When Catherine was named Princess of Wales, the media was quick to point out that she was the first person to hold the title since William's mother, Diana. It was inevitable that she would invite comparison to the late princess, but Catherine is anything but in Diana's shadow. Though she has always spoken with admiration and respect of her late mother-in-law, she has also shown her own ability as a senior royal time and time again. As the queen-in-waiting, she will be facing new challenges of her own, at the same time as supporting her husband and easing her son along the road to his own eventual succession, which likely won't be for many years to come. However, as both a mother, wife and working royal, her duties will be numerous and bring with them challenges of their own.

Of course, if tragedy hits the royal family, Prince George's succession may not be as far away as his family hopes. Though it hasn't happened for many centuries, should George succeed whilst still a child, the Regency Acts state that a regency must be established to ensure continuity of rule until the heir reaches the age of 18. Though the role of regent wouldn't necessarily fall to the Princess of Wales, she would certainly want to play an important part in helping her son navigate the role should he succeed whilst still a child. Though the possibility is remote, she must still understand constitutional and monarchical matters in case the worst happens.

ABOVE The key members of the royal family on the balcony of Buckingham Palace after the king's coronation

In the past, the royal family has faced criticisms about the perceived bloat amongst its ranks and about the exact status of some more controversial members of the Firm. In times of austerity, the public has understandably sought explanations as to who is considered a working royal, what duties they undertake and, crucially, what they cost. King Charles is believed to privately share such concerns and it's notable that the members of the family who played an official part in his coronation were minimal. It's understandable too that the Prince and Princess of Wales have been positioned front and centre at official occasions, as befits their status as the heir to the throne and his consort.

William and Catherine will be very aware indeed that the monarchy is increasingly a subject for debate, with republican sentiments being voiced with increasing fervour particularly at the time of the coronation. As the next generation of the house of Windsor, the future of the monarchy will ultimately fall to them and their own children in turn, and it is a responsibility that cannot be underestimated. Just as Charles is now the head of both the nation and the family, it is a role that will one day be assumed by the current Prince of Wales, with the Princess at his side. They will also be responsible for shaping and guiding the generation that will follow them, as their son, George, will one day succeed to the throne himself.

The current Prince of Wales has spent his entire life being prepared by his father and grandparents for the duty that awaits him. His wife benefitted from the guidance of the late queen for the first decade of her marriage and now, with the passing of Elizabeth II, she and her husband will take their lead and tutelage from King Charles III. Ultimately, however, whilst their path is to some degree dictated, the steps they take along that path are theirs to decide. They will make their own decisions, for better or worse, and one day shape the monarchy to their own intentions. It is without doubt a daunting responsibility and one that neither will take lightly. However, in a changing world, it is right that even the most historic of institutions should change too, and that includes the royal family. King Charles III has already begun the process of change and the next generation of monarchy will not only look back on past traditions, but forward to the future too. The world is a dynamic place that never stands still, and the Prince and Princess of Wales are keen to reflect this in their own family and interests. As King Charles III embarks on his own reign after seventy years waiting in the wings, he no doubt does so in the knowledge that the future of the house of Windsor is in the safest of hands.

RIGHT The Prince and Princess of Wales undertook many engagements in the lead up to the king's coronation

"The Prince and Princess of Wales have been positioned front and centre at official occasions"